A LOVE OF UIQ

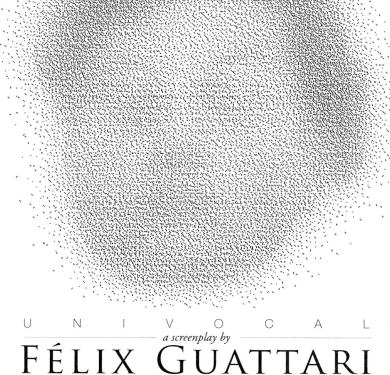

U N I V O C A L

a screenplay by

FÉLIX GUATTARI

Translation & Introduction by Silvia Maglioni and Graeme Thomson

Un amour d'UIQ
by Félix Guattari
translated by Silvia Maglioni and Graeme Thomson
as *A Love of UIQ*

© Editions Amsterdam, 2012
Published by arrangement with Agence littéraire Astier-Pécher
ALL RIGHTS RESERVED

First Edition
Published by Univocal
123 North 3rd Street, #202
Minneapolis, MN 55401
English Language Edition ©Univocal

Designed & Printed by Jason Wagner

Distributed by the University of Minnesota Press

ISBN 9781937561956
Library of Congress Control Number 2016930857

TABLE OF CONTENTS

I. PREFACE
Silvia Maglioni & Graeme Thomson

II. A LOVE OF UIQ
Félix Guattari

UIQ: Towards an Infra-quark Cinema (or an Unmaking-of)

by Silvia Maglioni & Graeme Thomson

I. Chaosmotic In(fra)ferences

Imagine an autopoietic entity whose particles are constructed from galaxies. Or, conversely, a cognitivity constituted on the scale of quarks. A different panorama, another ontological consistency.

The emergent self — atmospheric, pathic, fusional, transitivist — ignores the oppositions of subject-object, self-other and of course masculine-feminine.

Here then is an entity, an incorporeal ecosystem whose being is not guaranteed from the outside: one which lives in symbiosis with the alterity it itself contributes to engendering.

Félix Guattari, *Chaosmosis*[1]

---

1. Félix Guattari, *Chaosmosis: an ethico-aesthetic paradigm*, Sydney, Power Publications, 1995.

13

Everything could be rewritten, as the diary kept by Fred, the slippery journalist and writer testifies — a diary whose manuscript has been religiously conserved in an armoured vault by one of the superpowers — since with each new reading its statements are modified, the meaning of its clauses shifts.

This text, to be handled with pincers, might evoke the diary of Marie Curie, which like its author was irradiated to such a degree that even now it remains perfectly capable of mortally contaminating anyone who dares to read it without taking the necessary precautions.

Félix Guattari, *A Love of UIQ* (Preamble)

What's in a phrase? Reading Guattari's *Chaosmosis* for the first time back in 1995 when it was published in English, and struggling to grapple with terminology that initially resembled something akin to the technotopian prophecies of a cyberpunk novel, we most probably skipped, or trampled, oblivious, over much of the dense undergrowth of the prose. Trying to get the "general idea" of what Guattari wanted to say, we almost certainly paid only the scantest attention to any of his sentences. So much for singularities. Twenty years on, however, a number of those sentences now strike us with the force and depth of their compressed energies and resonances, as though several dimensions of the words we see in the text lie folded up like the volutes of a Calabi-Yau manifold, unable, perhaps on account of their instability or incompatibility with the existing universe's relation of forces, to explode or expand into being.

A casual, or even academic reader of *Chaosmosis*, would most likely attribute Guattari's references to astronomy, microbiology and particle physics to the sweeping range of his interests, his vastly eclectic reading and multifaceted, transversal thinking. Little would s/he suspect that behind them also lay a wholly other trajectory of desire and becoming, involving a collaboration with one of America's most radical independent filmmakers, a flirtation with Hollywood and seven years of conversations, letters, notes and rewrites that would crystallise into three versions of an ambitious science fiction screenplay, *Un Amour d'UIQ*, that was never filmed, but traces of which lie scattered in Guattari's subsequent writings and, it could be argued, in the tropes of later sci-fi cinema, a matter to which we will return.

UIQ, *l'Univers Infra-quark*, the Infra-quark Universe, the formless intelligence at the core (and periphery) of Guattari's script, is clearly the entity that lies behind the "cognitivity constituted on the scale of quarks" that we find, almost as an aside, in the pages of "Machinic Heterogenesis." Considered in terms of the film's proposed narrative arc, this is wholly apt, as we might imagine UIQ, after its misadventures in seeking visible human (and cinematic) form, returning to its former realm of the invisible and imperceptible. Yet, when viewed in this particular slant of light that streams from the unrecoverable past through dim archive windows to reflect weakly (UIQly) off the surface of badly xeroxed typescripts, barred from further reproduction by the lapidary stamp of a copyright notice, the "different panorama" to which *Chaosmosis* alludes might become inseparable in a reader's mind from the thought of the tripod or dolly that would make it concretely possible as a new horizon for Guattari to explore. As many of his friends will tell you, Félix always wanted to be a filmmaker.

Of course a detailed reading of the UIQ script shows that the sense of this "different panorama" may have extended to a rethinking of the cinema apparatus itself, through what Guattari was bringing from his experience as a schizoanalyst, his years working with Deleuze on the conception and writing of their mammoth *Capitalism and Schizophrenia,* his involvement in the Italian Autonomia movement and the birth of free radio as the political seeds of what he would call the Post-Media Era and his passion for transversality and infra-disciplinarity, not to mention his role in the experimental cinema and theatre workshops at La Borde. As an outsider to the codes of the movie business, he could envision a different kind of machinic arrangement for popular cinema, not only in terms of its complex of audio-visual techniques, effects and affects, but also, and perhaps more crucially, in its modes of production and distribution.

II. Cine-bacteria

Take a simple example: a patient in the course of treatment remains stuck on a problem, going around in circles, and coming up against a wall. One day he says, without giving it much thought: "I've been thinking of taking up driving lessons again, I haven't driven for years"; or, "I feel like learning word processing." A remark of this kind may remain unnoticed in a traditional conception of analysis. However, this kind of singularity can become a key, activating a complex refrain, which will not only modify the immediate behaviour of the patient, but open up new fields of virtuality for him: the renewal of contact with long lost acquaintances, revisiting old haunts, regaining self-confidence... In this, a rigid neutrality or non-intervention would be negative; it's sometimes necessary to jump at the opportunity, to approve, to run the risk of being wrong, to give it a go, to say, "yes, perhaps this experience is important." Respond to the event as the potential bearer of new constellations of Universes of reference.

Félix Guattari, *Chaosmosis*[2]

A number of semioticians believe they can shed light on unconscious mechanisms through the techniques of cinema. But rarely have psychoanalysts had the chance to express themselves by helming a film production.

This is the experiment I wish to attempt, not merely at the level of the film's narrative and psychological content, but equally in the fabric of perceptions and affects that is woven at every stage of its production.

Félix Guattari, *A Love of UIQ* (Preamble)

The story of UIQ is *pure* science fiction, beginning for us with a seemingly inert object, a file, buried in a remote archive, miles from anywhere yet harbouring strange powers, emanating an eerie fluorescent light, an energy field that will contaminate those who happen to lay eyes upon it, penetrating under the skin and working its way up into the brain, embedding itself into neural networks and taking hold of the decision-making apparatus through sheer force of will.

2. Félix Guattari, *Chaosmosis: an ethico-aesthetic paradigm, op. cit.*

At least that's how Guattari might have imagined it. This is no doubt the effect he would have liked the document to have when he presented it to the decision-makers at the Centre National de la Cinématographie in 1987, banking on the state funding that would enable him to produce *A Love of UIQ*.

Of course the idea that a militant thinker like Guattari might persuade a government funding body to bankroll a science fiction movie, a film that Guattari, with no previous filmmaking experience (in lieu of a filmography, the CV he attached to the application contained references to his being under police investigation during the Algerian war, his involvement in the 1977 Bologna uprisings and his links with Italian Autonomists like Toni Negri and Franco Piperno), was proposing to direct himself, was surely *in itself* pure science fiction.

To say nothing of the pitch for the film that he included in his director's Preamble, which set out such goals as exploring cinema's capacities as a tool for producing subjectivities or bringing to the screen the complex relation between individualized and machinic components, filming the various becomings (child, woman, animal, multiple, invisible) undergone by a group of characters who, despite their veneer of normality, were in fact to be considered "castaways of a new cosmic catastrophe." A catastrophe that, Guattari specifies, "is at the same time present and potential, imaginary and real, and whose actual presence draws its strength solely from its ability to empty the future of all consistency." The funding commission might have been forgiven for confusing parts of the Preamble with dialogue from the script itself. As though, through a kind of semiotic seepage, Guattari the director had become one of the characters. The screenplay had reached out to engulf its inventor, retro-fictionalizing him and casting him in the role of visionary leader of this band of cosmic castaways.

But how are we to specifically locate Guattari's own interests in, and approaches to, science fiction? How might they relate to his other published writings and his multiple roles in post-68 French intellectual and political life? How can we contextualise his desire to be a filmmaker, his need to *passer à l'acte*? We've already seen how UIQ is immanently present in the folds of *Chaosmosis*. But Guattari describes the character as having no limits in time or space, so UIQ is logically also a latency in his earlier

17

writings and practices, and most particularly in the dark matter of what fails to appear.

To begin with, if we can speak of a beginning, it's worth considering that before Guattari started working on the UIQ screenplay, he had already made a couple of notable attempts at screenwriting. In the first of these, *Project for a film on free radio*,[3] written around 1977, the events shadow Radio Alice's disruption of the state's broadcasting monopoly in the year of the Bologna uprisings. In Guattari's film, the action is shifted from Bologna to Turin, where Radio Galaxie is broadcasting in the midst of battles between protesters and police, relaying signals from the barricade strewn, tear-gas stained streets of the city. The film follows the errances of Elena and her "schizoid" companion Ugo as they try to reach the station headquarters, hitching a ride with a disillusioned stockbroker who quickly falls under the charming Elena's spell.

One interesting aspect of this short film — which Guattari imagined shooting on video in a loose, semi-improvised style, akin to that of Alberto Grifi — is the resonance he sets up between Radio Galaxie and the mindset of Ugo, neither of which recognises any clear boundary between sender and receiver. The permeability of the schizoid body as an indeterminate zone between inside and outside already constitutes one of the conditions of collective enunciation. In his Director's Notes, Guattari explains how he wanted to use one of the earliest portable video cameras, invented by his friend Jean-Pierre Beauviala. This camera, he implies, would permit a light, "free" cinema shot in the midst of events, capturing real-life processes while allowing space for improvisation and simplifying the workflow from filming to editing.

In Guattari's film, the radio station becomes the polyphonic mouthpiece of a hydra-headed movement that the state would try to frame as a form of malicious interference, an alien invader to be repelled, sending tanks into the streets to crush the uprising in scenes that recalled a *War of the Worlds*-type scenario. The advent of free radio was seen as a potential danger to the social order that had to be suppressed (Radio Alice was violently shut down in a police raid in March 1977) because it interfered

3. *Projet de film au sujet des radios libres* in Graeme Thomson and Silvia Maglioni (Eds.) Félix Guattari, *Un amour d'UIQ, Scénario pour un film qui manque*, Paris, Éditions Amsterdam, 2012.

not only with the official narrative of events but with the whole representative discursive framework that assigned the positions and delineated the divisions which regulated the speech of the social body. What made free radio so subversive was not merely the way it shattered the boundaries between transmitter and receiver, but equally the way it brought together different kinds of discourses that official channels rigorously strove to keep separate. In response to Artaud's call for a body without organs, the body of language and the organs of speech were thoroughly disorganized. Nothing of its type had ever been heard before through the type of "mass media" that could permeate both public space and the domestic environment. And the reaction was violent.

Autonomist politics, liberating itself from a crippling representative framework, was already a kind of science fiction, since it concerned the emergence and nurturing of new forms of life, ways of speaking, producing and relating to one another. As a voice from Radio Galaxie declaims (quoting an actual transmission from Radio Alice), in an inventive sequence where the broadcast would be transmitted through the car radio while filming took place in the middle of urban riots:

> To con-spire means to breathe together and this is what we are accused of. They want to stifle our breath because we have refused to breathe in isolation, each in their own asphyxiating workplace, their individualized family unit, their atomizing domicile.[4]

The Bakhtinian polyphony of Radio Alice and other free radio stations resulted both from the fact that they were many-voiced — constituting a media platform from which anyone could potentially speak — and that they briefly fostered multiple modes of speech and of DJing that gleefully trampled on the fences erected by institutions and identitarian microfascisms between different discursive fields and areas of expertise. Politics, poetry, philosophy, rock, history, news from the street and from

---

4. "Cospirare vuol dire respirare insieme e di questo siamo accusati. Vogliono toglierci il respiro perché abbiamo rifiutato di respirare isolatamente nel proprio asfissiante luogo di lavoro, nel proprio rapporto individualmente familiare, nella propria casa atomizzante." See *Collettivo A/traverso, Alice è il diavolo. Storia di una radio sovversiva*, Bifo and Gomma (Eds.), Milano, Shake Edizioni 2002. In English see "Radio Alice — Free Radio" in Sylvère Lotringer and Christian Marazzi (Eds.), *Autonomia: Post-Political Politics*, Cambridge/MA and London, Semiotext(e), 2007.

the factory floor, jokes, experimental music, erotic literature, militant songs, children's games, fairytales and free jazz were brought together in a movement of what Guattari would later refer to as machinic heterogenesis.

Could cinema, still a major force in the moulding of subjectivity with its mechanisms of projection and identification, attain a similar level of collective enunciation? Could one make a film on free radio that would also be a "radio film," as well as a "radiology" of society's hidden, suppressed or divided forces, without falling into the trap of a hypostatised representation?

Jean-Luc Godard had already attempted something of the sort in *Le Gai Savoir* (1968), which flirted with expanded notions of radio or TV broadcasting. Here, footage of the May '68 demonstrations, accounts of historical struggles, citations from writers and philosophers of different epochs and recordings of present day events are assembled on a single plane of "current affairs" reporting. These reports are interspliced with the musings of two young actors (Juliet Berto and Jean Pierre-Léaud, who would become a close friend of Guattari) appearing like molecules of proto-humanity set adrift in some pre-big bang cosmic night, as well as interviews with children (anticipating the format of *France, tour, détour, deux enfants...*) Through the sonic persistence of burbling and buzzing short-wave interference patterns, the film evokes the potentially intergalactic horizons of radio signals traversing space and time, secreting the alien tongues of revolutionary theory within their stochastic flux. However, such experiments, when not actually banned from wider circulation, were quickly ghettoized (even and especially by militant circles) as a type of eccentric and self-indulgent intellectual posturing, destined for extinction. *Chemins qui ne mènent nulle part*, they remain, like most of Godard's productions of the 1970s, as broken paths, untravelled byways of the history of cinema.

Yet perhaps Guattari — a stranger to the auteurial prerogatives that continued to haunt Godard's cinema even when he relinquished his own signature during the Dziga Vertov Group period — was more tuned into the collective dimension of enunciation to which free radio gave concrete form, and with this short film he was already projecting an alternative destiny for a minor cinema to come, as an affective relay of the Post-Media Era:

An essential condition for succeeding in the promotion of a new planetary consciousness would thus reside in our collective capacity for the recreation of value systems that would escape the moral, psychological and social lamination of capitalist valorization, which is only centered on economic profit. The joy of living, solidarity, and compassion with regard to others, are sentiments that are about to disappear and that must be protected, enlivened, and propelled in new directions. Ethical and aesthetic values do not arise from imperatives and transcendent codes. They call for an existential participation based on an immanence that must be endlessly reconquered. How do we create or expand upon such a universe of values? The suggestive power of the theory of information has contributed to masking the importance of the enunciative dimensions of communication. It leads us to forget that a message must be received, and not just transmitted, in order to have meaning. Information cannot be reduced to its objective manifestations; it is, essentially, the production of subjectivity, the becoming-consistent of incorporeal universes. [...]

The current crisis of the media and the opening up of a Post-media Era are the symptoms of a much more profound crisis. What I want to emphasize is the fundamentally pluralist, multi-centered, and heterogeneous character of contemporary subjectivity, in spite of the homogenization it is subjected to by the mass media. In this respect, an individual is already a "collective" of heterogeneous components. A subjective phenomenon refers to personal territories — the body, the self — but also, at the same time, to collective territories — the family, the community, the ethnic group. And to that must be added all the procedures for subjectivation embodied in speech, writing, computing, and technological machines.[5]

In another remarkable sequence of the projected free radio film, the car becomes a sort of mobile camera traversing urban space (as it does in the long driving sequences of Danièle Huillet and Jean-Marie Straub's *History Lessons*). In a fog of tear gas, Elena gets out to look for a phone to transmit a report to Radio Galaxie. We see her silhouette from a distance, in a public phone box, as the sound of her voice comes through the car radio. Once again the idea is to film the street in real-time with the radio as its soundtrack. In this way, the fictional scenario could potentially

5. "Remaking Social Practices" in Gary Genosko (Ed.), *The Guattari Reader*, Oxford, Blackwell Publishers, 1996.

insinuate itself directly into the flux of events, while the "industrial" timescale of cinema production could be circumvented thanks to the lightness of the equipment and a crew working outside the structures of professionalization.

Compared to the experimental mappings of 1968, a "radiology" of 1977 might have shown a wider, more disjunctive convergence of emancipatory energies. While in Italy the Autonomia movement was reclaiming life from the Fordist factory regime, in Britain, where molecular political shifts tend to find their most immediate expression (and recuperation) in pop culture, punk had unleashed the dystopian refrain of "no future." As Bifo writes:

> The 1977 movement — in its colourful and creative Italian version and in its British one as well, which was punk, gothic and disturbing — was founded on one intuition: desire is the determining field for every social mutational process, every transformation of the imagination, every shift of collective energy. It is only as a manifestation of desire that we can understand the workers' refusal of the wage relation, of conforming their lives to the timing of the assembly line, realized through absenteeism and sabotage. [...] The workers' disaffection for industrial labour, based on a critique of hierarchy and repetition, took energies away from capital, towards the end of the 1970s. All desires were located outside capital, attracting forces that were distancing themselves from its domination.[6]

However, it may be overstating the matter somewhat to say that "all desires" were outside of capital. Certainly the massive popularity of *Star Wars* in 1977 would suggest otherwise. As well as effectively curtailing the political aspirations of the New-Hollywood *auteurs*, this fable of supposedly popular rebellion against imperial domination was symptomatic of another, more sinister "no future" to come, that of postmodernism and its implicit rejection of modernism's "progressive" historical narrative. In the guise of science fiction, a genre for a long time allied to or foreshadowing the trajectory of modernity, *Star Wars* presented a retrogressive fairy-tale of the triumph of US-style Western individualism and its harnessing of the eternal, immaterial *force* of capital, while the vaguely medieval aristocratic genealogy of

---

6. Franco Bifo Berardi, *The Soul at Work - From Alienation to Autonomy*, Los Angeles, Semiotext(e), 2009.

the Jedi knights hinted at the emerging corporate neo-feudalist aspect of its imminent restoration.

Around 1979, two years after *Project for a film on free radio*, Guattari began collaborating with Robert Kramer, who was later to become an important creative partner in the development of the UIQ script. Kramer had recently settled in France, after completing *Scenes from the Class Struggle in Portugal*, and Guattari was a great admirer of his movies *Ice* (1969) and *Milestones* (1975), both of which resonated with what he had written on the subject of group micropolitics. If *Ice* posed the question of the potential molar rigidity affecting militant movements engaged in armed struggle, *Milestones* traced the mutation and dispersion of countercultural energies towards more molecular, intimate and self-seeking roads of emancipation, while at the same time seeking to situate US freedom struggles within a more complex and contradictory historical framework.

Together, Guattari and Kramer sketched out an idea for a film on the Italian Autonomia movement, *Latitante*, about two Italian women fugitives with a child in tow, gone to ground in France. The outline for the film drew upon Guattari's ongoing involvement in helping radical Italian intellectuals find refuge in France after being scapegoated as the *cattivi maestri* of the movement. But equally important was Kramer's desire to capture the day-to-day reality of the Autonomists' experience. With the mounting repression of protests and the arbitrary persecution of militant figures came a need for a more underground, molecular politics. The atmosphere of heightened paranoia, together with a growing sense of exhaustion and ambivalence towards collective action, unsurprisingly gave rise to cinematic narratives of flight, dissembling and disappearance. But it was also a time of great solidarity and friendship, as a letter from a mysterious Jean in prison (possibly Genet), included in the *Latitante* film dossier, testifies:

Resistance has isolation inherent in it. You are opposing yourself, your fragile mind and delicate body, to the enormous weight of things-as-they-are, conditions systematically defended by vast power. As an individual you crash into all the traditional bonds and codes and networks that are the matrix of things-as-they-are. If you are alone (I'm sure we will be alone from time to time — this right now is a lucky time!) it takes every ounce of will to survive, to stay sane, to not break (or foolishly try to break out!).

And in this context the bonds among resisters grow and deepen. They have to, it is the secret glue, the secret fire, it is a source of energy that unites and sustains the strivers. Sometimes I feel the ideas as such are sitting on top of this volcano.

We cannot as yet formulate and systematize the fires raging deep inside this land. They manifest themselves directly in the behaviour, in feelings. But the time will come when we understand what is happening here, and see that we have given birth to a whole, different way of seeing and experiencing things; that we have given birth to a new body of ideas.[7]

Promising an uneasy though alluring melding of fiction and documentary, *Latitante*, which was to star Pasolini's icon Laura Betti as one of the women fugitives, with Guattari and Kramer themselves in supporting roles, would have been an interesting addition to the cycle of films — from Fassbinder's *The Third Generation* (1979) and Rivette's *Le Pont du Nord* (1981) to Godard's great sequence of films *Sauve qui peut (la vie)*, *Passion* and *Prénom Carmen* — that was to mark a kind of drawn-out *Schwanengesang* of post-68 political cinema in Europe. And indeed, perhaps at this stage Guattari and Kramer's idea of a new kind of molecular political cinema was preparing its own flight, looking for a "safe house" where it could go to ground and regroup its forces.

In the poetically pragmatic opening notes to the film dossier (the style is obviously Kramer's), Guattari and Kramer lay out their proposed approach to filming the fugitives' world:

---

7. Graeme Thomson and Silvia Maglioni (Eds.), Félix Guattari, *Un amour d'UIQ, Scénario pour un film qui manque*, op.cit.

24

This movie is not an exercise in search of an interpretation. On the other hand, its very basis is an assumption about the complexity, the very ambiguity of its subject. We can think of our approach to the subject as that of a laboratory technician taking samples of cells from different organs of the organism.

Or as a radiologist taking X-rays from each relevant angle:

X-rays of the chest show shadowy bones,
a ghostly heart,
all the strands of an organism of great capacity
efficiently compressed into two dimensions.
Only intimacy knows this thick blood
forcing through its channel,
livening, lightening human dreams,
the hot secret food
that carries in its spiral codes
the lessons of all our striving ancestors.[8]

One is immediately struck by the references to scientific investigation and experimentation, particularly in the field of microbiology, as well as the implied search for a revolutionary genetic code transmitted down though the ages. It is under these circumstances that we can imagine the autonomist "cells" of a radio-logical film begin to change into bacteriological ones, the chloroplasts of a mutant strain of phytoplankton functioning as a relay to what would emerge as UIQ, the Infra-quark Universe.

This genre shift was also symptomatic of a larger reorientation of the political imaginary between the late 1970s and early 1980s, which, following the repression of social struggles on the ground, seemed to undergo a gradual detachment from the world and its material conditions towards more remote horizons of the possible.

In many films of this period, the unconscious mourning and yearning for other forms of life, briefly promised by the countercultural revolutions, was re-projected in infantilizing, conservative terms of a transcendental — even messianic — horizon of benevolent extra-terrestrial visitors and alien intelligences (*Close Encounters of the Third Kind, E.T.*) or more subversively

---

8. Graeme Thomson and Silvia Maglioni (Eds.), Félix Guattari, *Un amour d'UIQ, Scénario pour un film qui manque*, op.cit.

transformed into horrified fascination, whether with a monstrous other (*Alien*), viral contagion (*Shivers, Rabid*) or mutations in subjectivity produced by technology and media (*Videodrome*).

In *A Love of UIQ*, the alien intelligence would take the form of an invisible, infinitely small universe that is already immanent, present as a potential force at the quantum level of the infra-quark — insisting as a kind of dark matter that simply requires an adequate relay to be able to manifest itself and insinuate its way into the organic life and machinic arrangements of our planet.

III. Something for the UIQ-end(less)

Aspects of this kind of polysemic, animistic, transindividual subjectivity can equally be found in the worlds of infancy, madness, amorous passion and artistic creation. It might also be better here to speak of a proto-aesthetic paradigm, to emphasise that we are not referring to institutionalised art, to its works manifested in the social field, but to a dimension of creation in a nascent state, perpetually in advance of itself, its power of emergence subsuming the contingency and hazards of activities that bring immaterial Universes into being.

Félix Guattari, *Chaosmosis*

Doubtless the notes which we hear at such moments tend, according to their pitch and volume, to spread out before our eyes over surfaces of varying dimensions, to trace arabesques, to give us the sensation of breadth or tenuity, stability or caprice. But the notes themselves have vanished before these sensations have developed sufficiently to escape submersion under those which the succeeding or even simultaneous notes have already begun to awaken in us. And this impression would continue to envelop in its liquidity, its ceaseless overlapping, the motifs which from time to time emerge, barely discernible, to plunge again and disappear and drown, recognised only by the particular kind of pleasure which they instil, impossible to describe, to recollect, to name, ineffable — did not our memory, like a labourer who toils at the laying down of firm foundations beneath the tumult of waves, by fashioning for us facsimiles of those fugitive phrases, enable us to compare and to contrast them with those that follow.

Marcel Proust, *A Love of Swann*[9]

At the beginning of the film, this universe is no more than a faint signal in a sample of mutant cyanobacteria that the chronobiologist, Axel, has managed to smuggle out of a laboratory in Brussels. Wanted for acts of "terrorism" (the radio and TV interference caused by UIQ's early signals are immediately identified as such), he escapes to Frankfurt with the help of Fred, an American journalist. The film's opening scene sees their hijacked Piper Malibu touching down in a field, whose blackened clumps of earth absorb the colour of the frost that covers them in patches. The landscape is glacial, bloodless, bathed in a strange inconsistency. We are in the middle of the Winter Years.

> I am among those who lived the 1960s like a spring that promised to be never ending: no wonder I've found it so hard to adjust to these long winter years of the 80s. History sometimes dispenses gifts but it takes no prisoners, playing its hand without concern for our hopes and disappointments. So it's better to just get on with it and not bet too heavily on the natural return of the seasons. Especially when there's no guarantee there won't be a new autumn to follow or a winter even harsher than this one.
>
> And yet part of me continues to hold onto the idea that somewhere, hushed preparations are being made for future encounters with new waves of collective generosity and inventiveness, and with an unprecedented will of the oppressed to get out, try to hold back the deadly and deadening politics of the powers that be and redirect economic and social activity to more human, less absurd ends.[10]

Such hushed, semi-clandestine preparations form the motor of the kind of cinema Guattari envisions in *A Love of UIQ*, intended as a molecular, collective practice which, even as it partakes of the depression that underlies the false euphoria of the emergent 1980s image culture, would constitute a laboratory to counter its

9. Marcel Proust, *Remembrance of Things Past: I*, London, Penguin 1983, p.228
10. Félix Guattari, *Les années d'hiver*, Paris, Les Prairies Ordinaires, 2009 [our translation].

most toxic effects by fostering intensive gestures and signs of life. An eternal return of the state of nascence.

This is also one of the reasons why the image repertoire of the film should, on the surface, so faithfully replicate some of the most clichéd aspects of 1980s cinema. We see this in the ambience of the disco-bar, on the edge of town, where Axel meets the punkish Janice, who will offer him and Fred shelter in the squatted factory building she shares with her fellow "castaways." At first, the scene is familiar from a hundred straight-to-video thrillers, while making nods to *Blade Runner* through Axel's peeling of a boiled egg and execution of an extravagant backflip. What is unusual, however, is the way these secondary signs are brought to the fore as the film's primary matter of expression, together with the machines in the bar, in particular the pinball machine around which the characters converge, as though they have begun to possess an excessive animistic vitality that choreographs the scene and leads the dance. The scene gives us one of the first clear signs of the UIQ effect, the volatile contamination it will instigate between the human, animal and machine realms.

Another is the elaborate jerry-built multi-screen interface that the squat's inhabitants help Axel construct, after overcoming their initial diffidence, to help him re-establish contact with the universe he has discovered — to which they give the name UIQ — and translate its interference signals into words, sounds and images with which it can communicate. As cables, screens and other devices proliferate, simultaneously connecting and separating the different portals permitting contact with UIQ, the building begins to look as though it is in the grip of a giant octopus, while the space secretes myriad sonic and gestural micro-refrains that, like Vinteuil's *petite phrase*, will eventually expand to contaminate the surrounding environment.

Part of the inventiveness of *A Love of UIQ* lies in the way Guattari deploys the squat scenario to recast his own transversal practice — with its mix of clinical, political, philosophical and aesthetic components — in terms of a multi-layered fabulation. The disused factory — peopled by its odd mix of social outcasts — constitutes a heterogeneous, idiorhythmic milieu bearing certain similarities to the psychic economy of La Borde, while the disturbances that UIQ's signals cause in Hertzian waves slyly reference the strategies of the free radio activists Guattari had met in Italy.

In the virtuoso sequences where Axel (described as an amateur acrobat "who in launching his body into the air, evokes the way UIQ turns towards humanity") slips his seemingly gratuitous gymnastic feats into the conversation without breaking sweat, he does so in a manner that suggests a whole new possible cinematic choreography of body, voice and language.[11] Then, there is the question of UIQ's own machinic "body" and subjectivity which, having no form, no temporal and spatial limits, nor a stable sense of identity, tends to parasitize existing forms of life and machines, infiltrating the minds and bodies of its hosts and plaguing communications systems with its interference and scrambling of codes.

However, it isn't long before UIQ begins to manifest itself as a proto-facial diagram composed of three black holes, an image that haunts TV screens and can appear indiscriminately in the sky, pools of water, or the movement of crowds or the flight of birds. The process of subjectivation it undergoes in the squat effectively lures UIQ into adopting more human personality traits. Though it continues to constitute a deterritorialized field of contamination — affecting machines, communications systems and living organisms — UIQ also acquires distinct characteristics: a bearing, a voice, a manner of speech (eerily close to Guattari's own). Its discovery or invention of a sense of "self," thanks to the nurturing guidance of Janice, who has the task of informing it about sexuation and identity, causes it to fall in love with her, while her body becomes a conduit for its own feelings and provokes fits of jealous rage when she occasionally abandons her role as its teacher for more conventional physical pleasures with Axel.

As Janice steers it towards a limiting, potentially dangerous sense of hetero-normative male self-identity, she becomes the object of its fatal passion, an impossible love that will have catastrophic consequences for both them and the planet. Its

---

11. As well as the obvious reference to Pris in *Blade Runner*, here we can see (pre)echoes of Cronenberg's *The Fly* and Leos Carax's *Mauvais Sang*. We can also assume that scenes like this were not a rare occurrence at La Borde, as the documentary *Le droit à la folie* (Igor Barrère, 1977) testifies. In this observant portrait of everyday life at Cour-Cheverny, we see the methods of Guattari and Oury at work in the perpetual self-invention of a collective, though heterogeneous, machinic ecosystem.

attempts to conquer her take on a surrealistic dimension when it (now a "he" in the script) tries to incarnate itself as a man, Bruno, only to find the embodied self becoming a physical rival for her affections. Here too Guattari departs from the familiar science fiction template where the alien, when it is not actively hostile, might represent an ideal para-religious embodiment, rather than a disastrous *mise en abyme*, of an emotion such as love.

In a sense, UIQ is nothing more than the formless *between-ness* that connects its numerous botched avatars and that subtly alters relationships among the squat's residents, many of whom develop their own singular rapports with the universe: Manou, a precocious and highly independent child apparently without parents; Steeve, a burnt-out computer scientist; Eric, a schizoid young man with a penchant for washing machines (a development from Ugo, in the free-radio script); and, crucially, Janice herself, who transforms from a punkishly impertinent university dropout and amateur DJ to a figure of tragic grandeur, a cyborg Joan of Arc, the stubble-headed shell to UIQ's ghost. Her sudden disappearance, following a raid on the squat by an anti-terrorist task force, condemns the bereft UIQ to an infinite — because bodiless — pain, and unleashes his rage in the form of a plague of genetic mutation, turning huge numbers of people into semi-amphibians who are, as a result, in constant need of hydration. Only when Janice returns and agrees to have the UIQ virus implanted into her brain, does the plague end. However, the cerebral merger with UIQ brings with it an undesired immortality, as she discovers when subsequently attempting suicide in the last scene of the film.

But before this, much of the central part of *A Love of UIQ* is given over to exploring the effects that UIQ and the squatters have on each other and on the outside world, an attunement process that gives rise to a bizarre choreography of inexplicable gestures, actions and micro-events where we are never quite sure who or what is the cause, where one will or desire ends and another begins.[12] Everything seems to take place in an elastic,

12. Guattari's abiding interest in the non-linguistic components of semiotic polyvocality is also present in another film project he briefly sketched out in the 1980s, "Project for a film *by* Kafka", a process in which ideas for the scriptwriting and filming, focusing on the gestures, postures and latent sounds of Kafka's expressive machine rather than its more narrative elements, were to have been generated by a series of workshops involving

indeterminate space of tragicomic burlesque where it is impossible to make any clear distinction between subjects and objects of perception, vision or sensation. Hence the film's bizarre, unsettled tonality, the way it tries to release the impersonal or transversal semiotic delirium that subtends science fiction cinema from the signifying structures (story, psychology, clearly individuated characters etc.) that plug it back into normative patterns of desire.

Countering this movement within the script's own diegetic framework is the international commission — whose suavely aloof president, with his penchant for cream cakes and treating the phenomenon of UIQ like a plate dropped in a restaurant, seems like a character stolen from Chabrol — and, within the squat itself, the teenage couple formed by Antoine and Michèle, the only inhabitants who have any contact with the outside world, through their precarious McJobs as motorbike couriers, and who remain unaffected by UIQ's influence.

Antoine and Michèle function like the film's exterminating angels. Harbingers of a coming normalization, Guattari describes them as standard-issue junk food consuming teenagers and they seem to reflect his growing despair about the processes of a depoliticizing subjectivation that were already underway in the 1980s as Europe's youth fell under a globalizing spell of MTV and US high-school culture and its approval-seeking refrains.[13] There is a slightly bitter irony in the fact that Antoine's name should also evoke Truffaut's Antoine Doinel, whose frozen childhood gaze looked forward towards the coming insurrection of May '68. It is Antoine and Michèle who will precipitate the events leading to the squat's discovery and destruction and to UIQ's revenge.

It is perhaps within the codes of the spectacular, however, that the film is at its most subversive, almost as though UIQ itself had taken the director's chair. The numerous elaborate set-piece scenes enchain actions and affects that veer wildly across registers

---

participants from different fields including choreographers, actors, musicians and architects. See *Projet pour un film de Kafka* in Stéphane Nadaud (Ed.), Félix Guattari *Soixante-cinq rêves de Franz Kafka,* Paris, Lignes, 2007.

13. We refer here particularly to the spate of popular teen movies predominantly set in high-school environments (from John Hughes comedies such as *Pretty in Pink* and *The Breakfast Club* to Robert Zemeckis' *Back to the Future*) which dominated the box office during the mid 1980s and whose narratives of surface rebellion typically concealed and insinuated repressive Oedipal desiring structures, though it might also be argued that *Back to the Future* was partly a satire on such a reactionary movement.

and genre boundaries, which, like UIQ, seem to have no sense of measure or proportion.

A potential air disaster at a crowded beach resort, triggered by UIQ's failed attempts to copy a keyboard melody played by Manou (in a satirical lo-fi re-working of the climactic scene of *Close Encounters of the Third Kind*) is envisioned with the mixture of dreamy wonder and gleeful malevolence of a child's game, only to then mutate into a mixture of surreal comedy and poetic suspension, as though a scene from *Ivan's Childhood* had drifted onto the set of *Les Vacances de Monsieur Hulot*.

Elsewhere, sexual decorum is radically overturned when a traumatized UIQ's disembodied black-hole diagram of a face, appearing on several different screens, reacts like a disgruntled baby in witnessing a primal scene of "parental" congress between Janice and Axel. Wracked by the physical sensations of the couple, UIQ's face assumes the contorted expression of each in turn,[14] until it utters a desperate animal cry whose unbearable intensity is relayed through the petrified body of Eric, perched like a Greek statue on a chair, and the antics of a screaming monkey that in the end defecates on his shirt.

In a later scene, we see UIQ on one screen engaged in intimate dialogue with Janice, while on another it gives precise instructions to Manou on how to prepare a deadly cocktail to give to a tramp she is afraid of, who dwells in the recesses of the squat — an episode that distantly evokes a scene in Rossellini's *Germany Year Zero*, in which Edmund's unrepentant Nazi schoolteacher convinces him to poison his weak father.

As the film progresses, we have the feeling of snatched intensive fragments from an eclectic repertoire of filmic references, from *Close Encounters of the Third Kind* to *Theorem*, to the aforementioned *Blade Runner* and *Mauvais Sang*, being re-fashioned as components of a more unruly, deterritorializing machine, one in which the elements of voice, body and face undergo a startling recomposition,

---

14. The morphing of UIQ's face in this scene anticipates that of the aquatic alien presence in James Cameron's *The Abyss* (1989) which, faced with the estranged couple of scientists, likewise assumes the shape of each as they look at it in turn, but in a purely visual, mimetic manner, designed mainly to illustrate the efficacy of the effect and the technology which produces it.

a world where Godard, Tarkovsky, Pasolini and Fellini trade ideas with Cronenberg, Carpenter and Lynch.[15]

Though we may never know what form *A Love of UIQ* would take on screen, it's tempting, even within the spectacular tropes of a sci-fi blockbuster, to imagine certain sequences being close to silent cinema — which, in Guattari's view, had been much more successful than sound cinema in expressing the intensities of desire in relation to the social field, since the signifying script (and with it the individualising forces of capitalism) had not yet taken full possession of the image. The notion of a clear-cut separation between different regimes of cinematic image is by no means clear. It is a question of how desire flows and is channelled, both within and between the regimes. As Guattari wrote in 1977, in one of his most lucid texts on minor cinema:

> Desire is constituted before the crystallization of the body and the organs, before the division of the sexes, before the separation between the familiarized self and the social field. It is enough to observe children, the insane, and the primitive without prejudice in order to understand that desire can make love with humans as well as with flowers, machines, or celebrations. It does not respect the ritual games of the war between the sexes: it is not sexual, it is transsexual. [...] I must say of cinema that it can be both the machine of eros, i.e. the interiorization of repression, and the machine of liberated desire. There is no political cinema on the one hand and an erotic cinema on the other. Cinema is political whatever its subject; each time it represents a man, a woman, a child, or an animal, it takes sides in the micro class struggle that concerns the reproduction of models of desire.

> The real repression of cinema is not centred on erotic images; it aims above all at imposing a respect for dominant representations and models used by power to control and channel the desire of the masses. In every production, in every sequence, in every frame, a choice is made between a conservative economy of desire and a revolutionary breakthrough. The more a film is conceived and produced according to the relations of production, or modelled on capitalist enterprise,

---

15. Thinking about contemporary directors whose work shows an affinity with the wild veering between, or cohabitation of genres we see in Guattari's script and in its seeming disregard for narrative coherence or verisimilitude, we should also mention the cinema of Jean-Claude Brisseau, in particular *De bruit et de fureur* (1983) and *Les Savates du bon Dieu* (1998).

33

the more chance there is of participating in the libidinal economy of the system. Yet no theory can furnish the keys to a correct orientation in this domain. One can make a film having life in a convent as its theme that puts the revolutionary libido in motion; one can make a film in defence of revolution that is fascist from the point of view of the economy of desire. In the last resort, what will be determinant in the political and aesthetic plane is not the words and the contents of ideas, but essentially asignifying messages that escape dominant semiologies.[16]

In this sense the UIQ script constitutes a somewhat paradoxical, quasi-object. Rather than providing the coherent structure required for it to be green-lighted for production, it opens up a problematic field that promises to undermine the codes of mainstream spectacle while saving (or spending) the a-signifying delirium that subtends it, which it hopes to place in the service of *another economy of desire*. But because of this wild semiotic expenditure, it can never settle upon a specific code of its own. Like UIQ itself, Guattari's film resists hypostatisation in a stable form or identity.

IV. A Huge Ever Growing Pulsating Brain
That Rules from the Centre of the Infra-World

I told him that realising a potential always attracts me less than the unrealised, and I mean not only the future but also the past and missed opportunities. It seems to me that our history has been that every time we have fulfilled some small part of an idea, we are so pleased that we leave the much greater remainder unfinished.

Robert Musil, *The Man Without Qualities*[17]

16. Félix Guattari, "Cinema of Desire" in *Chaosophy — Texts and Interviews 1972-1977*, Sylvère Lotringer (Ed.), Los Angeles, Semiotext(e), 2009. Original French text "Le cinéma : un art mineur" in *La Révolution moléculaire*, Paris, Éditions Recherches, 1977.
17. Robert Musil, *The Man Without Qualities*, London, Picador, 1995, p.297.

I'll have to make the effort to translate telegraph signals — to translate the unknown into a language I don't speak and without even knowing what the signals mean. I shall speak that sleepwalker's language that would not be a language if I were awake.

Clarice Lispector, *The Passion According to G.H.*[18]

This shifting, unsettled quality, figured in UIQ's own problems of *embodiment*, of finding a form it can inhabit, traverses the development of Guattari's script, which evolved through three very different versions. With UIQ, Guattari had invented something that surpassed, or passed under, its proposed frame of representation, an infra-cinema that despite, or perhaps on account of, its remaining unmade, insisted by way of a kind of intermittent pulsation. In this sense, the three successive revisions of the screenplay can almost be read as records of an overall pattern of UIQ's own manifestations and disappearances.

In the first version, co-written with Kramer around 1980-1981, much of the action takes place in a hi-tech hippie commune, somewhere in the eastern US. It seems that Guattari originally intended Kramer to direct the film, and that he wanted to produce it in Hollywood. The fact that Guattari sent a copy to the office of Michael Phillips, the producer of *Taxi Driver* and *Close Encounters* who, though intrigued by some of the ideas, deemed the project "too political" for the US,[19] shows that his aim at this point was to make the film as *minor cinema on a major scale*. Perhaps he and Kramer were hoping to subvert the Hollywood machine from within, liberating spectacular images and sounds from the normalizing shackles of conventional narrative by pushing those narrative devices to an absurd extreme (with the risk of falling into parody).

Their differences in approach to the story are nonetheless striking, as Kramer's letters to Guattari and his notes make clear:

---

18. Clarice Lispector, *The Passion According to G.H.*, London, Penguin, 2014.
19. See Dialta Lensi Orlandi's letter to Guattari from August 3rd 1982, as well as Hollywood synopsis and related production documents in Graeme Thomson and Silvia Maglioni (Eds.), Félix Guattari, *Un amour d'UIQ*, op.cit.

I worked on your story outline, trying to continually imagine 'how can we tell this story so that we can see most of it, so that it isn't dependent on verbal exposition.' As you will see, this has led to various changes, some of them are quite important (Elimination of long period of experimentation in communication with UIQ for example).

The commune is not mentioned, but that is only because we will have to figure out how to create this ambience. It is not directly related to 'story.'[20]

While Guattari insists on the importance of the collective milieu as a territory for experimenting with processes of subjectivation — a territory that would additionally enable him to further scramble the codes of cinematic representation through the insinuation of elements of performance, dance, installation and video art — Kramer imagines the whole story taking place in flashback from the point where UIQ has already merged with the girl's consciousness (in the first draft she is called Bernadette), as a kind of fragmented, psychogenic fugue in which we no longer know to whom or to what these memory images belong.

What I'm concentrating on now is the form, the different parts of the whole. I sort of like the structure that is beginning to emerge: large and open and broad, and more and more focusing in on Bernadette until we enter the tunnel of her final communications with UIQ, a dream-psychotic-subjective-obsessive tunnel of quickly moving mental events. We start at the edge of the sea and finally enter the whirlpool.[21]

Kramer clearly wishes to throw the spectator off balance, filming the mental events of a subjectivity invaded by a universe without spatial or temporal limits, an entity without psychological constancy or a clear sexual orientation. In this scenario, the events of the squat should only appear as memory flashes deprived of a coherent point of remembrance. Such a mise en scène might make us think of Alain Resnais's *Je t'aime, je t'aime* and his depiction of the shattered memory of a man (Claude Rich) who

20. Robert Kramer, Letter to Félix Guattari, 27.1.1981, in Graeme Thomson and Silvia Maglioni (Eds.), Félix Guattari, *Un amour d'UIQ*, ibid.
21. Robert Kramer, Letter to Félix Guattari, date unknown [early 1982], ibid.

believes himself to be responsible for the death of his wife (Olga Georges-Picot), as he tries to reconstruct his past with the aid of an experimental time machine constructed by a team of government scientists. Except that here the subject who remembers, or who dreams, is also the object of the memory or desire of an other (or several others). This psychotic passage of the subject who becomes the other in itself might also be compared to the cinematic universe of Alain Robbe-Grillet, with its incommensurable repetitions of neighbouring presents. One can easily imagine the deranging power of a similar vision brought to bear on a sci-fi blockbuster.

A second, unfinished version of the script (also co-written with Kramer and dating around 1983) transfers the action to a France of the (then) near future, where an integrated Tativille-style complex with shopping, media, banking, sports, entertainment and social rehabilitation facilities — all accessed by digitally encoded personal swipe cards — sets out the coordinates of a nascent control society amid the emerging networked infrastructures of Mitterand's Paris.

The third and final version, written by Guattari himself around 1986-1987 — the most underground in style, which we have decided to publish here — alludes to the TAZ, the squat culture of 1980s Germany and to the dystopian post-punk aesthetic of films such as Muscha's *Decoder* (1984) or Ossang's *L'affaire des Divisions Morituri* (1985). Nonetheless, more than to any specific cultural context or regime of representation, UIQ seems to pertain to the realm of contagion and contamination. Its existential dilemma lies in the continual translation of the unknown language of its universe into a series of unstable forms, none of which can be final. In quantum terms, wave function has the advantage over particle, and process over product.

This is one of the reasons why the script, in its *désœuvrement*, constitutes such an unusual document on the border of Guattari's oeuvre, one that it would be unfruitful to relegate to a pile of marginal *disjecta*. Like UIQ's own subjectivity, it is both a work in progress and a potentially infinite series of discarded versions. And, like the fractal machines in *Chaosmosis*, what UIQ traverses are substantial scales. And it does so in engendering them. But the existential ordinates that it invents were always already there.

"How can this paradox be sustained? It's because everything becomes possible (including the recessive smoothing of time, evoked by Rene Thom) the moment one allows the assemblage to escape from energetico-spatio-temporal coordinates. And, here again, we need to rediscover a manner of being of Being — before, after, here and everywhere else — without being, however, identical to itself; a processual, polyphonic Being singularisable by infinitely complexifiable textures, according to the infinite speeds which animate its virtual compositions.[22]

Similarly, as a piece of writing *A Love of UIQ* occupies a paradoxical double, or even multiple temporality: while as a text by the author known as Félix Guattari it may seem to possess a certain "formal identity," as a movie script, desiring to be transformed into a film, it is an entirely provisional document destined for endless rewritings, modifications and betrayals — what, were it not for capitalism and its prerogatives, would become a collective enunciation.

Translating the text, this presents us with a dilemma: should one treat the task of translation here as that of conveying, in as far as it is possible, the exact sense of the author's words, or should one consider it in its provisionality, as something the process of translation, being one of the links in the long chain of film production, will inevitably transform? Should we see the text in its becoming film? And if so, what film? What are the implications of translating a script that was never published of a film that was never made, some thirty years after it was written? Perhaps it's useful to return to Walter Benjamin's essay "The Task of the Translator" when he writes: "Just as the manifestations of life are intimately connected with the phenomenon of life without being of importance to it, a translation issues not so much from the life of the original as from its afterlife."[23] In the case of *A Love of UIQ*, what we have is a work whose life is in some sense "all afterlife" (or perhaps pre-life), and at its heart an entity whose possibilities of existence are founded entirely upon endless translation.

Our approach in this translation has been twofold. Where Guattari's cinematic vision is at its strongest and most acute, in his wonderful descriptions of gestures, expressions, spaces and

22. Félix Guattari, *Chaosmosis: an ethico-aesthetic paradigm, op. cit.,* pp.50-51.
23. Walter Benjamin, *Illuminations*, London, Fontana Press, 1992 [translation modified].

atmospheres and in his visions of the film's many elaborate set-pieces, we have translated more or less literally and with reference to the period in which the film is notionally set, the 1980s. However, we have on occasion seen fit to modify the dialogues slightly, in order to tighten their rhythm and convey more fully their desired spirit of insouciance and irreverence. Another motive for such reshaping is to get closer to the situation Guattari imagines for the film — that of the geographically displaced inhabitants of a Frankfurt squat — who would have included American, French, Danish, Italian, German and Infra-quark exiles whose interactions in the movie would most probably be in some form of English. We have taken some pleasure in trying to convey what the minorized English of this crew might sound like, to say nothing of that of UIQ itselves.

Post-Script — Towards an Ecosophy of the Unmade

Feelin' capable of seeing the end
Feelin' capable of saying it's over...

Chvrches, "Tether"

G. D. Is it a film?
M. D. It would have been a film.
(*Pause*)
Yes, it's a film.

Marguerite Duras, *Le Camion*

It's often the smallest scraps of evidence that are the most intriguing. The derisory, orphaned fragment is where desire is most likely to arise. Take this letter from Félix Guattari to Michelangelo Antonioni:

Dear Sir,

I asked our mutual friend Ugo Amati to send you the outline of a science fiction screenplay I've written, *A Love of UIQ*.

I would really appreciate it if you had the time to read it and it would be a great joy for me if you should be interested in becoming involved.

I've merely unfolded some key ideas that will have to be developed in more detail. Should the project be of interest to you I would be more than happy to meet you to discuss it in person.

Yours sincerely,
Félix Guattari[24]

We don't know whether Guattari ever sent the letter, or when it might have been written. Why would he have kept a copy? But as Axel says in the UIQ screenplay, "What happens to communications isn't necessarily the most important thing." So we decided to treat it as a signal, a transmission from some distant galaxy to another, possibly even more remote, that got lost in the quantum post.

One thing is more or less certain. While Guattari began working on his screenplay, Antonioni was completing what was to be his last major film for the cinema, *Identification of a Woman*. In the final scene we see the protagonist, a filmmaker navigating between a creative crisis and a stalled relationship, facing the sun with his eyes closed. After the vicissitudes of the story, he finally seems in a state of relaxation, dreaming of a science fiction film he will probably never make, an exploratory voyage into the heart of the solar furnace that, he hopes, will reveal mysteries of the universe. The idea is visually resumed in a deceptive lo-tech special effects sequence showing the spaceship — a converted asteroid — being sucked into a pulsing, yellow-orange deliquescence. As it recedes from view, the asteroid's twin engines appear to stare back at us like two slightly comical black-hole eye-sockets that eventually solarize into what look like the slits of a *settecento* Venetian half-mask. The asteroid-ship then vanishes into the sun's yellow core that gradually reveals itself to be the ghostly impression of an eye in extreme close-up.

24. Félix Guattari, *Un amour d'UIQ*.

40

A meditation on the conditions, possibilities, and limits of seeing and knowing, of vision and the visible, the film might well have struck a chord with Guattari and his ideas about an invisible alien intelligence from a subatomic realm even smaller than quarks, though he was likely also thinking of *L'Avventura* and the way its disappeared central character, the palindromic Anna, continues to dominate the film in her absence, like a kind of weather.

The prospect of a collaboration between Guattari and Antonioni is tantalizing, opening onto yet another possible avenue of UIQ's transformation. But fascinating as these lost horizons may be, it was the simple act of reading the screenplay, when we discovered it in the IMEC Archives,[25] that made the film already exist for us, as though by a kind of contamination. And this was in a way entirely consistent with the nature of UIQ, an entity with no clear limits in time or space that comes into being only through its parasiting and imitation of already existing forms of matter and energy.

By the time we published the script in France in 2012 with Éditions Amsterdam, in a volume we designed and edited ourselves, and wrote in collaboration with writer and psychoanalyst Isabelle Mangou, which also included the early film projects, as well as notes, production documents and fragments of Guattari's exchanges with Kramer, we had projected the film in our heads countless times. Nonetheless the cineastes in us wouldn't let it lie, even if we may have felt the script was inherently unfilmable. But how to convey something of this flickering vision and of UIQ's own instability and intermittence? Perhaps by finding ways to "produce" the film and manifest its universe without actually filming it.

An essay by Pasolini, "The Screenplay as a Structure that wants to be Another Structure", suggests that an unmade screenplay can constitute a genre of writing in its own right, one that potentially offers the reader a more active and collaborative role than does the novel.[26] But who is to say that a screenplay is merely a structure,

---

25. The Guattari and Kramer Archives are both preserved at IMEC, L'Institut Mémoires de l'Édition Contemporaine (The Institute for Contemporary Publishing Archives) at the Abbaye d'Ardenne, in Saint-Germain-la-Blanche-Herbe (France).
26. See Pier Paolo Pasolini, "The Screenplay as a Structure that wants to be Another Structure" in *Heretical Empiricism*, Indiana University Press, 1988.

or that its *desire of becoming* leans solely in the direction of the film to be? Especially in the case of a screenplay containing an entity such as UIQ, might it not also desire other forms of being?

This is why, instead of trying to film Guattari's script, we set about conceiving a number of manifestations of the Infra-quark Universe (performance, radio trailer, installation, fabulation, rumour...) that would function through the years in the manner of a relay: each partially taken up by others and given a new twist. They eventually led to an experimental essay film, *In Search of UIQ* (2013), which formed something of a cartography of this spatiotemporal continuum of non-realisation. As the title suggests, the film is a search, and as such it remains in that zone of uncertainty, in the towardness of what Pasolini calls the notebook film. *Not* towards a film.

However, the script still seemed to require further investigation, its almost thirty years of lost time called for a more collective vision of its infra-possibilities (and perhaps still does). In a series of gatherings held in seven European cities, to which we gave the name "seeances", we extended the idea of the film as a process, looking at Guattari's screenplay in a way that reflected UIQ's own predicament as an entity whose becoming has to be negotiated through ongoing translation and transduction. We considered how the subject of *A Love of UIQ* folded upon the question of the script's unending desire to become a film, or perhaps something else. Transduction can refer to any process by which a biological cell converts one kind of a signal or stimulus into another. More specifically, it concerns the transfer of viral, bacterial, or both bacterial and viral DNA, from one cell to another using a bacteriophage vector.[27] The idea here was to make Guattari's film exist by a process of contamination, with the screenplay functioning as a *cinebacteriological vector*, transferring the film and the Infra-quark Universe *in potentia* to a community of seers, or "envisionaries." Rather than a cinematic production that would reduce the indeterminate matter of UIQ to a specific set of representations, exploitable as a spectacle, the film would come into being through its unworking or worklessness,[28] as a living process of variations.

---

27. See Gilbert Simondon, *On the Mode of Existence of Technical Objects*, Univocal Publishing, 2016.
28. See Maurice Blanchot's discussion on the concept of *désœuvrement*.

These temporary communities (in a vague mirroring of the squat dwellers who make contact with UIQ) gathered around the screenplay and welcomed UIQ into their systems through the medium of the script, envisioning the film and the universe it unveils in relation to the specific cultural, political and linguistic context of their own existence and desires, their fabulated histories and futures, sometimes transposing the script's characters, actions and events to the present day. This work of transduction added further complexity to the work by which a written screenplay is normally *translated* to the screen. By conflating the roles of writer, director, actor and viewer, the envisionary communities were able to expand the territories of the film both from within and without, multiplying its narrative and affective folds, blurring the borders between the actual and virtual projection. Which also meant that the UIQ effect might have been there in the room, with and between them. People would start to feel the space and each other's presence differently, their tone of voice would change, something in the atmosphere shifted, though it was difficult (and perhaps undesirable) to identify exactly what this consisted in.

Our sense of time, but also of purpose and of efficacy, would change during these sessions, which became like zones of autonomous temporality in which the unknown quantity and intensity of vision displaced and devalued the currency of knowledge. And as we went on with the seeances, we began to realise we didn't need to rely so heavily on the script itself. Sometimes just the suggestion of a situation or scene was enough to set imaginations in motion. Plus there were aspects of the script that some people didn't find particularly fruitful or that they wanted to take in another direction, queery, alinguify, defacialise, infrathin...

With the sound recordings of these sessions, bearing in mind the screenplay and UIQ's potential desire for other becomings, we decided to make an invisible film by other means,[29] a polyphonic soundwork where all the voices, visions and spaces of gathering could co-exist, resonate, feed off and build upon each other. In the beginning, the idea was simply to "recompose" Guattari's film through glimpses of what had been evoked or speculated upon by the more than seventy envisionaries, but during the mixing

---

29. See Pavie Levi, *Cinema by Other Means*, Oxford University Press, 2012.

43

process, when we started to work on spatializing the voices, we and our mixing engineer noticed another "film" emerging in parallel to UIQ: the portrait of this scattered community coalescing across an acousmatic plane of collective enunciation and coming into some kind of being of its own.[30]

Perhaps this is what we would wish for Guattari's film, that it keep on existing in a quantum space, both wave and particle, process and crystallization, in an eternal return of nascence, but one that through its "infra" dimension may continue to produce a becoming ancestral, animal, vegetal, cosmic of the image, "collective entities half-thing half-soul, half-man (half-woman) half-beast, machine and flux, matter and sign" that are "always to be reinvented, always about to be lost."[31]

30. The soundwork was first installed at The Showroom, London, as part of our exhibition "it took forever getting ready to exist: UIQ (the unmaking-of)", February-March 2015.
31. Félix Guattari, "The New Aesthetic Paradigm" in *Chaosmosis*, op.cit.

A LOVE OF UIQ

SYNOPSIS

We're always wondering whether there might be life or intelligence on other planets, way up in the stars ... but we never ask ourselves about the infinitely small ... maybe it could come from there, from a universe that's even smaller than protons, electrons, quarks...

This is how Axel, a young biologist in his early 20s, reveals to Janice (a student dropout of about the same age) the amazing discovery he has just made.

But as soon as a device is installed to establish permanent contact with this mysterious entity, a major problem arises — a problem that led to the failure of Axel's previous experiments: though infinitely small, this Universe is capable of causing grave disturbances to Hertzian communications systems!

What follows is a series of spectacular convulsions all across the planet, a situation that only becomes stable once the inhabitants of the squat where Janice lives have managed to make verbal contact with the entity, which they have taken to calling UIQ (the Infra-quark Universe). This leads to a phase of reciprocal learning and exchange between the two worlds. But if, for their part, the small band of squatters comes to acquire extraordinary knowledge and capacities for action, the Infra-Quark Universe, with its infinitely superior intelligence, gets very little out of its dealings with humanity. On the contrary, it undergoes a shock whose result will be catastrophic, its discovery of "love" in its evolving relationship with Janice — a discovery that will eventually overturn and reshape the entire planet.

Unlike traditional science fiction models, what we have here is a Universe that, though all-powerful and prodigiously intelligent, is completely helpless when confronted with human realities such as beauty, sensuality, jealousy, and love... This leads to the creation of a new type of character, a manifold entity that calls into question the very notion of the individual.

While on the surface this screenplay may be read as a graphic novel, at another level it addresses questions of a philosophical, psychoanalytic or even psychiatric nature. Lastly, it gives visual form to a series of speculative hypotheses about the world we inhabit.

Preamble

I am a writer and psychoanalyst, as well as a director of a psychiatric clinic that employs methods of Institutional Psychotherapy.

Now I would like to direct what, at least in appearance, will be a science fiction film. This, no doubt requires some preliminary explanation.

A Love of UIQ, the screenplay I present here, is neither an autobiographical film nor an essay film, though it closely relates to my conception of psychoanalysis.

Years spent practising a psychotherapy of psychoses have led me to question traditional definitions of the unconscious, which treat it as a separate realm of the psyche, cut off from the social field or from artistic creation and accessible only to specialists. Contrariwise, it appears to me that the life of the unconscious is inseparable from the means of reading and analysis that give us access to it. Such means are themselves in continual evolution, and are particularly susceptible to being diversified and enriched through the contribution of new information and communications technologies.

The key thing for me in an analytic procedure, therefore, is to forge an original system of expression, a specific cartography suited to the singular figure of a subjective problem.

So in a way for me this film is a form of self-analysis. The intense work of drafting several versions of a screenplay was already an analytic experience that I would qualify as processual. Bringing it to the screen with the aid of cinema professionals and the participation of artists like the painter Matta and the composer Ryuichi Sakamoto will allow me to carry this process further.

I particularly look forward to working collectively on the fabrication of "new images." Cinema is an extraordinary instrument for producing subjectivity. Up until now its rapports with psychoanalysis have been complex and frequently conflictual. There are films that have been made about psychoanalysis and psychoanalytic themes just as there has been a desire to interpret films, often abusively, in a psychoanalytic light.

A number of semioticians believe they can shed light on unconscious mechanisms through the techniques of cinema. But rarely have psychoanalysts had the chance to express themselves by helming a film production.

This is the experiment I wish to attempt, not merely at the level of the film's narrative and psychological content, but equally in the fabric of perceptions and affects that is woven at every stage of its production.

Félix Guattari

Principal Objectives and Themes

In this film I wish to explore a theorem about the current status of subjectivity, which posits that it consists of two kinds of components that are always intermingled:

1) An "ego" subjectivity, crystallized upon individual characters living in a kind of commune and who, though apparently normal, might be regarded as castaways of a new type of cosmic catastrophe, one that is at the same time present and potential, imaginary and real, and whose current presence draws its strength solely from its ability to empty the future of all consistency. On the other hand, this catastrophe corresponds to different phases of my own affective development, to a certain "choice of objects" that remain in suspension: becoming child, becoming woman, becoming animal, becoming multiplicity, becoming invisible.

From the outset, I ask the members of the commission to bear in mind that certain thematic elements, though essential, can only be crudely sketched out in the writing of a script like this. Such is the case for the main character that the community will itself become, whose taking form will require a particular stylistic visual and spatial treatment that will not become apparent until the stage of shooting and *mise en scène*. Here, perhaps more than in any other domain, the image, the imaginary and the creativity specific to the event will reveal their indivisible nature.

2) A machinic subjectivity — hyper-intelligent and yet irredeemably infantile and regressive — framed in an entity called UIQ, *Univers Infra-quark* (the Infra-quark Universe), that has no fixed limits and no consistent persona nor a clear psychological or sexual orientation. The intrusion of this "machinic" unconscious dimension into ordinary subjectivity will produce significant upheavals.

The drama evoked here runs parallel to the one our societies are currently undergoing, where the rise of computerized forms of thought, sensibility, imagination and decision-making, the digitization of a growing number of material and mental operations, is not always easy to reconcile with the existential territories that mark our finitude and desire to exist. In the film, this contradiction will be brought to its climactic point with the dramatic failure of UIQ's attempt to incarnate itself in the character of Bruno.

But in the end this final impasse regarding the question of finitude and singularity can only serve to illustrate a fact self-evident to classic psychopathology, that is to say that a psychotic love can never durably pin its alterity to a fixed identity, nor even to a stabilizing process of identification of whatever nature.

So is the prodigiously intelligent software and molecular super-power that is UIQ destined to come off the rails of its existential avatars, like a needle skidding across a badly scratched record or like the harrow of the machine in Kafka's penal colony carving away at the skin of the condemned?

As for the film's heroine, having allowed herself to be drawn into the incestuous game of the passage to transcendence, she is now condemned to drift eternally outside the realm of human communication and affect.

Who is responsible for the final tragedy?

Nothing was decided in advance and in truth, as far as the contemporary world is concerned, the question remains entirely open. Everything could be rewritten, as the diary kept by Fred, the slippery journalist and writer testifies — a diary whose manuscript has been religiously conserved in an armoured vault by one of the superpowers — since with each new reading its statements are modified, the meaning of its clauses shifts.

This text, to be handled with pincers, might evoke the diary of Marie Curie, which like its author was irradiated to such a degree that even now it remains perfectly capable of mortally contaminating anyone who dares to read it without taking the necessary precautions.

"Give us back our death" could be an alternative title for the film. And yet, no! To whom could such a plea be addressed? It will never be the same person who answers your call!

MAIN CHARACTERS[1]

AXEL:

Around 20-25. Of German origin. A bizarre, unpredictable character, forever elsewhere. Axel, A biologist and amateur acrobat who — in launching his body into the air — evokes the way UIQ turns towards humanity.

FRED:

In his forties. An American journalist and all-round handyman. In the first part of the film we gather he is in the service of a number of shady political powers, none of which is made explicit, but as in real life, it's clear from the way he behaves. As the story unfolds he becomes a kind of witness to present events or more precisely to a present that expresses the future.

JANICE:

20-25. Not exactly beautiful. More solid, compact, mysterious and somewhat aristocratic as her Italian origins would seem to indicate, archaic traits that for her signify a need for the absolute. At first she appears like a kind of prototype of an *Elle*

---

1. There exist several different character descritpions which vary in terms of age, nationality, etc. Here we have chosen to publish the most detailed version of these.

61

woman, ready to resolve her emotional and relationship problems by going to bed with the first guy she sees.

MANOU:

7 or 8 years old. We don't know where she comes from. Manou invents her own forms of expressing herself outside of speech. She appears strangely adult-like and sure of herself.

ROBERT:

A kind of updated Jean Gabin. Affable, if a bit temperamental and macho with it, he once worked as a cook on a nuclear submarine. If for Stein "a rose is a rose," for Robert "an omelette is an omelette." Nothing prevents him from going deeper but it's of no interest to him. Nature is as nature does and he could just as easily have sex with Janice or Eric. To him there's no difference, the orgasm is the same, why make a big deal of it.

STEVE:

In his 40s. African-american. Elegant. A former NASA engineer, he collects rare documents on Dostoyevsky for a data study.

ERIC:

Danish. At the same time violent and incredibly gentle. Schizoid. Gifted with a prodigious imagination, he is in some sense Janice's alter ego.

FRANCIS and DOMINIQUE:

Phantasmic projections of Eric's mind that may appear at any time, giving his imagination concrete form.

ANTOINE and MICHÈLE:

Around 14. They have left their provincial hometown in pursuit of an American dream that they project onto the city. Physically, they resemble standard-issue junk-food consuming teenagers in leather jackets and astronaut-style motorbike helmets. They speak a hyper-modern argot borrowed largely from American slang, have Madonna posters on the walls etc. They work for a motorbike delivery service and carry walkie-talkies. Precariously employed, part of the black economy, they seem to be the only ones living in the squat who have any contact with the outside world. They are also completely impermeable to the "outsider" UIQ. All this should appear to be the consequences of adhering to an artificial lifestyle based on advertising models. Clean and polite but fundamentally hollow, they'll no doubt end up serving behind a counter. They don't know it but the audience does!

JENNIFER:

She seems ageless, she could be anything from 60 to 35. Her face is marked by the centuries and by the silence of one who is unaware of what she knows. Eurasian, her mere presence explains the community's existence as a point of no return. Jennifer is "beyond," in a certain sense, she is beyond even UIQ. We won't see much of her, mainly just hear her inimitable voice intoning a wordless chant, soft and guttural, evoking a silence fraught with mystery. Perhaps it is she that Janice will hear when she is condemned to deathlessness.

BRUNO:

Enigmatic and emblematic. Imagine God entering into contact with the world and assuming a human form...

63

UIQ (the Infra-quark Universe):

Unlike traditional science fiction models, what we have here is a universe that though all-powerful and prodigiously intelligent is completely helpless when confronted with human realities such as beauty, sensuality, love... This can lead it to episodes of infantile regression similar to petit bourgeois reactions of jealousy, envy or blackmail...

A LOVE OF UIQ

Field – Ext. – Night

It's winter, at the twilight hour said to lie between dog and wolf. An unreal atmosphere. Clumps of blackened earth absorb the colour of the frost that covers it in patches.

Wisps of marbled air rise over the field, mirroring it in bizarre continuity.

A landscape bereft of horizon, drained of colour, bloodless, glacial, bathed in a strange inconsistency.

We hear the engine drone of a small plane before it becomes visible, flying at low altitude.

Plane – Int. – Night

Inside the cabin the pilot anxiously scrutinizes the luminous dials on his instrument panel. He checks his flight plan and turns on the radio handset.

PILOT
This is Malibu calling Frankfurt II, Malibu calling...

A brusque hand cuts the contact, leaving the pilot appearing taken aback momentarily. The hand belongs to a guy in his fifties, Fred, whose black leather jacket reinforces his burly physique.

FRED
Forget the control tower, this is our stop.

PILOT
Are you crazy?

With the gesture of a police detective, Fred flashes a card in the pilot's face.

PILOT
What are you. Some kind of cop?
(*He reads the card*). Wait a minute, that's a press card.

FRED (*with a snigger*)
Don't you know journalists hold all the cards?

He thrusts the hand in his gun pocket, the pilot momentarily takes fright, but instead of a weapon he extracts a wallet stuffed with dollar bills. With calculated slowness, he lobs a wad of fifties onto the instrument panel, then a second and a third; on the fourth, a sudden jolt knocks all the money to the floor. The defeated pilot bends to gather it up. Fred helps him, nonchalantly using his shoe like a croupier's rake. We catch this shamefully crouched figure casting an anxious glance towards the rear passenger compartment. A limp body occupies one of the four seats, the body of a young man with his head and upper torsoe slumped over the armrest. Below him a small monkey jumps around tugging at his drooping locks.

FRED
That kid is probably more important than the rest of us five billion monkeys put together.

(*To the monkey*) Leave him alone, Lara.

The monkey jumps back onto its master's shoulder as he limps, stiff legged, towards the passenger seat. Carefully he rights the young man's body, cradling his head protectively.

FRED
Axel, can you hear me?

No response. The journalist sweeps Axel's hair back from his forehead and runs his fingers through it. A handsome face, despite the dark circles under the eyes, which are closed. The plane rolls into a turn as the pilot prepares to land. Axel's eyelids open, he looks around but makes no response and drifts back into unconsciousness.

The wheels hit the ground hard, jolting the plane this way and that before it finally comes to rest.

The pilot shouts over the noise of the engine.

PILOT
Hurry up and get the hell out of here.

FRED
We'd be quicker if you gave me a hand.

PILOT
Oh, I'm sure a journalist like you can handle it.

Fred gives him a contemptuous shrug and reaches for the lever to open the door. The icy blast of air that greets him sends a shiver through his whole body as he peers out at the dense sheet of mist floating above the field. The monkey perched on his shoulder begins to tremble. He bundles her under his jacket.

Axel's seat is empty. The shock of the landing has knocked him to the ground. At first all we see are his two bare feet. Fred grabs hold of them and drags his body towards him. He is wearing only a sweatshirt and jeans. To protect his head the journalist grips him from underneath the arms.

Fred, his bag, the monkey and Axel are hardly out the door when the pilot slams it shut and revs up the engine. The plane taxis off and disappears into the fog.

Opening music and credits

The strange spectacle of the lame journalist dragging Axel through the mist.

Main Road – Ext. – Night

Night has fallen by the time Fred reaches the field's edge. We hear the sound of traffic coming from a main road a little way below them.

Exhausted, Fred lets go of Axel, careful to slip his bag under the young man's head as he slumps to the ground. Sweating profusely despite the cold, he wipes his face and neck with a handkerchief. He inspects their surroundings before deciding to leave Axel alone, heading off in the direction of a service station whose lights he has seen some hundred yards or so farther down, on the other side of the road. Unable to make a dash across the heavily trafficked highway, Fred forces a passage between the oncoming drivers, causing them to brake and veer dangerously to avoid him. The air fills with the sound of angry car horns. Axel sits up to see what's gong on.

72

Service Station – Int. – Night

In the station shop, the racks of gadgets, car accessories and sweets lie deserted. Strangely, all the customers are huddled round the cash register. Anxiously, they listen to a newsflash from a transistor radio.

VOICE-OFF SPEAKER
...This is Dieter Magen of Radio Frankfurt. The radio interference that has been affecting transmissions these last few weeks is finally over. It was in the suburbs of Brussels that a NATO special task force discovered the pirate installation...

FRED (*under his breath*)
Discovered! Blew the place sky high more like!

VOICE-OFF SPEAKER
...Unfortunately the terrorists managed to make their getaway before police arrived on the scene. It's still not known how the group operated, or on whose behalf. Meanwhile the federal Government and the International Investigation Commission are renewing their appeal to the public to report any suspicious behaviour...

Fred picks up a packet of biscuits that he tears open as he walks over to a telephone booth. He lifts the receiver and slips a card into the machine. Checking no one is listening he digits a number.

FRED
Hello? Associated Pictures and Press? I need to speak to Neil Baster. Tell him its urgent...

Fred slips a biscuit under his jacket. The monkey reaches out to grab it.

FRED
Hello, Neil, is that you? Thanks for the holiday tip buddy...
But it's a bit too hot for my style.

NEIL (*off*)
Where are you, Fred? Give me a number?

FRED
Those assholes almost wasted us. But I managed to get him out
of there, and for now we're in the clear.

NEIL
He's with you? Where the hell are you?

OTHER VOICE-OFF (*creepy*)
Tell us your location Mr. Newman.

FRED
What is this? Who are you? Put Neil on, goddammit.

NEIL (*off*)
Hey Fred, I'm sorry. They got me locked down on this one.
We can't let him go. So why don't you be a good boy and tell
us where we can come and get you.

FRED
Forget it. You know I don't do that dance. I'm a journalist not
a cop!

NEIL (*off*)
I don't think you realize what you're dealing with here. You are
in shit that is black-hole deep, my friend.

FRED
Listen I have pictures and I have Europe's most wanted. If you don't print, well we'll just have to let the bidding war commence.

NEIL (*off*)
You're fucking crazy. You don't know what's at stake!

FRED
I told you I never ever devil with the deep blue C. Your choice. Take it or lose it.

OTHER VOICE OFF (*with cool menace*)
We can have you arrested, Mr. Newman, you're about to step into a world of inconvenience.

FRED
Yeah, but right now all you can do is go fuck yourself.

Furious, he hangs up and walks out the door.

Service Station – Ext. – Night

Fred is about to cross back over the road when out of nowhere appears a three-wheeler van stacked high with wooden crates. It narrowly avoids running him over and he starts back when he sees that it's Axel who is driving. Axel, still groggy with sleep struggles to keep his eyes open, as the van zigzags and crashes into a trash can, stalling the engine. Fred leaps on board, pushes Axel into the back, and takes the wheel.

Main Road – Ext. – Night

The three-wheeler traverses housing estates, clutches of low build-ings that seem to have sprouted up on the desolate terrain vague of the city's edgelands. Irritated by the tomato crates, Axel begins jettisoning them onto the road.

FRED
Stop doing that, are you crazy, you're going to give us away!

AXEL
Give away. Huh. Huh. And what did that asshole want. Hey, I'm talking to you. What do you want from me?

FRED
Trust me; okay?

AXEL
That's cute. He knocks me unconscious and it's supposed to inspire my trust.

FRED
Would you prefer I handed you over to the feds? It won't take a minute.

AXEL
Whatever, *hombre*. It's your call. Just find me some shoes … my feet are cold.

Hypermarket – Int. – Night

The customers, mostly couples, glide up and down the aisles to the muffled strains of muzak.

Behind one of the rows of shelves we discover Axel seated on a stool. Crouching awkwardly, Fred helps him try on a pair of training shoes.

Axel, making no effort to help Fred, studies him with a mocking air.

FRED
Not too tight? Stand up, see how it feels.

Axel gets up and wiggles his feet inside the shoes.

AXEL
They're a bit on the clown side.

FRED
They'll have to do, we've no time to lose.

He picks up the box, tucks it under his arm and makes for the checkout.

Realising that Axel isn't there, he turns round and sees him some way back, shuffling forward like an ancient Chinese lackey, his oversized training shoes still laced together.

Frankfurt – Ext. – Night

The three-wheeler crosses the city centre where the streets and houses have been rebuilt in the same style as before the WWII allied bombardments.

At a crossroads traffic light, Axel starts to bark loudly at the monkey. Panicked, it tries to bite him. Fred manages to separate them.

The lights turn green. The three-wheeler stalls.

Exasperated honks from the cars stuck behind, unable to overtake. Fred tries the ignition several times but to no avail.

FRED
Out, move.

He grabs Axel by the sleeve. They slip out of the vehicle and down a side road, leaving the traffic blocked at the junction.

AXEL
Where are we going?

FRED
A friend's place, where we can lay low.

They come to an enormous square dominated by electronic billboards. Several police cars are clustered around one of the buildings, blue lights flashing.

FRED
About-face, quick...

Club – Int. – Night

A cacophony of noises floods the disco bar, a melange of dance music, video game sounds and rowdy conversation.

The place is populated by an odd, multi-ethnic clientele, a mix of jobless youth, drug addicts and other marginals, many of whom are turned towards the DJ, Janice, a superb young punk, who visibly rules the place. A guy approaches her, seizes her from behind. She pushes him away.

GUY
What is it with you?

Janice shrugs her shoulders with a knowing sigh. Then, spotting a young guy, Helmut, she smiles at him and signals him to join her. Helmut gets up and forces his way through the crowd towards her. She grabs him by the collar and kisses him, flashing a defiant look at some other would-be suitors, before changing the record and dragging him onto the dance floor. She dances with flair while he struggles to imitate her moves.

JANICE
What are you doing after?

HELMUT
After what?

The rejected suitor goes back to his table.

GUY
That bitch!

His remark is greeted by titters of laughter. Then something happens to change his aggressive demeanour.

GUY
Who's that just walked in?

Axel has just appeared in the doorway.

OTHER GUY
Never seen him.

Behind Axel, Fred hesitates to enter the bar.

FRED
Careful, I don't think this is our kind of place...

Axel rolls his eyes and crosses the room to the bar where he plucks a boiled egg from a bowl. He starts to unpeel it and nonchalantly ambles over to a pinball machine.

Looking extremely uncomfortable, Fred tries his best to fade into the background. He takes a seat at a corner table.

Axel swallows the remains of the egg in one gulp and signals to Fred that he needs change to play. Fred reluctantly gets up.

FRED
You could move your own derriere. I'm not your personal assistant.

He gives him a few coins and takes an uneasy look around the room.

FRED
I don't intend to hang around here long. This place is unhealthy.

AXEL
Hey, feel free. This isn't a cop show. I don't need you to have my back.

He starts to play. Fred goes on staring at him silently.

AXEL
What are you looking at, are you a nance or what?

Looking vaguely ashamed, Fred steps back and bumps into Janice.

JANICE
Piss off grandad.
(*To Axel*) Do you mind?

Without waiting for an answer, she pries his hands from the pinball machine and takes his place.

Still on the dance floor, Helmut observes the scene. He looks slightly peeved.

Janice plays with great dexterity.

AXEL
700,000 ... 800,000 ... 2,000,000! This chick is amazing!

As though to underline his enthusiasm, he executes a dangerous backflip. Janice, nonplussed, stops playing.

The whole room is now looking at them.

FRED (*to Axel*)
Come on, show's over. We're out of here.

AXEL
What are you talking about? This is the shit, man! The girl has definitely got game.

He inserts another coin in the machine. Janice thanks him with a wink and beckons him to join her.

JANICE
Where you from? Not from around these parts, that's for sure...

AXEL
Not exactly, I'm Belgian.

Enraged, Fred gives the pinball machine a hefty kick. Everything stops.

JANICE
Who invited this freak?

Fred seizes Axel firmly by the arm and drags him outside.

AXEL
Hey, that hurts.

Janice slides between the tables to rejoin Helmut. She whispers something in his ear. He tries to embrace her but she slips away.

JANICE
Be nice and take over, will you... Do it, please, for me...

Club – Ext. – Night

Fred tries to force Axel away from the club.

FRED
Fucking moron!

AXEL
You need to take a chill pill padre.

FRED
You are really whacked. These bars are crawling with feds. That girl...

AXEL
Her? No way.

JANICE
Hey guys! Where's the party?

She dons a jacket and runs to catch up with them.

AXEL (*grabbing her by her jacket collar*)
I thought it was at your place.

(*He casts a glance in Fred's direction*) We have a small problem, you feel me?

JANICE (*with a complicit air*)
I feel you.

A taxi appears. Janice flags it down. They get in. Not wanting to be left behind, Fred reluctantly follows.

Taxi – Int. – Night

JANICE (*to the driver*)
24, Oberstrasse.

DRIVER
Where's that?

JANICE
North Ringsturmen.

DRIVER
I'm not going there.

JANICE
Move it, don't be a pain.

The driver says nothing, just drives. Janice and Axel strike up a conversation.

JANICE
Belgian you say?

AXEL
Yeah, from Brussels.

JANICE
They say things are kicking off up there.

Fred gives Axel a swift and violent kick.

JANICE
And what do you do?

AXEL
What do you mean *do*?

JANICE
I mean in life.

AXEL
Nothing much. Aside from a bit of biochemistry. And you?

JANICE
Well, you saw me.

AXEL
Ok, but what are you … a student?

Janice
Yeah like philopsychosocio lalalology, that kind of shit. Eugh, what's that monstrosity?

She indicates the monkey that has just defecated on the seat.

JANICE (*to Fred*)
Do you mind wiping your brat's ass?

DRIVER
Hey, what's that godawful stink back there?

Fred takes a Kleenex and wipes up the mess.

Janice whispers something in Axel's ear, who responds likewise. She bursts into a fit of giggles.

FRED (*to Axel*)
Would you cut it out!

JANICE
Oh so now he's not allowed to talk to strange girls, ladies of the night. What are you gonna do? Send him to bed without any supper?

She grabs Axel by the neck and kisses him full on the mouth. We see the car streak down an empty road and disappear into darkness.

Street off the Ringsturmen – Ext. – Night

A wheel sinks into a hole in the road's broken surface. The taxi stops.

DRIVER
This is as far as I go.

He flicks the switch to release the centralised door locks. Janice gets out, followed by Axel.

FRED
Hey, wait for me!

The driver turns round, brandishing a sawn-off shotgun. Fred quickly gets out his wallet and offers him a banknote. Still gripping his weapon in two hands, the driver signals with his chin to put the money on the front seat.

DRIVER
Put it there! There! Keep your hands where I can see them!

FRED
Easy!

DRIVER
I told you, I told you I'd had it with the Ringsturmen! You know what the Ringsturmen is? A bunch of whores, crackheads, monkeys, Jews, ragheads is what the Rignsturmen is.

Fred gathers up the monkey, slips it under his jacket and gets out of the taxi.

FRED
Yeah well, so long!

The driver puts down his gun.

DRIVER
Goodnight sir. Thanks anyway.
(*He points up the road*) Oh, no. No. 24's up that way.

FRED
Sorry?

DRIVER
Over there … see?

The wheel revs before coming unstuck from the hole, causing the taxi to skid violently as it reverses. The driver swings the car around and out of sight.

A desolate wasteland of crumbling factory buildings. The area seems completely deserted.

Distant metallic rumbling contributes to a vaguely menacing atmosphere. Following the taxi-driver's indications, Fred walks up the road. We hear the soles of his boots crackling the gravel.

At number 24, he pushes open a rusty iron grille and enters a courtyard piled up with old barrels, crates and metal girders...

The courtyard is bordered on three sides by semi-dilapidated hangars that Fred proceeds to explore with a torch. In the one at the furthest end he spies a metal staircase which he mounts, moving stealthily. Through a skylight on the first floor he sees there is another building hidden behind the hangar: sheets are hung out to dry on a terrace.

Fred redescends, looking for an entryway. He hears someone cursing. In the beam of his lamp appears the ravaged face of a drunken tramp, lying amid piles of empty cans and bottles.

FRED
Sorry!

The man mutters incomprehensibly.

FRED
How do you get to the other side?

The drunk picks up a bottle and flings it in his direction. The bottle narrowly misses Fred and smashes against the wall.

A short while later, Fred comes upon a passageway leading to another courtyard, completely different from the first, with flowerpots, a portico and a swing. Everything here is clean and well-ordered.

He is standing in front of a well-kept industrial building whose only ground-floor door is locked. The windows are not too high, however, and Fred is able to hoist himself up onto a window ledge. With an effort he slides open a glass pane and hauls himself inside...

Factory – Int. – Night

A child's cry resounds through the building. The monkey escapes, bounding through the room. A door opens and the light goes on. Janice appears.

JANICE(*to a little girl*)
Don't be afraid, there's nothing to be frightened of. He's an American.

MANOU
Do we know him?

JANICE
Yes, yes, we know him.

On one side of the immense space where they are standing is a partitioned corner-room for the little girl, while on the other is a hammock where a bearded forty-something man lies snoring.

ROBERT
Turn that bloody light off!

JANICE (*to Fred*)
Try to make less noise. Here, this way.

FRED
Is Axel there?

JANICE
Oh yes, your scoop is here. Don't worry!

FRED (*shocked*)
What did he tell you?

JANICE
Tell me? Of course he tells me things, it's natural, don't you think. Now that we know each other, now that we're going steady!

Fred, agitated, looks around. He makes a lunge at the monkey but it's too quick for him.

All three leave the room, passing to an adjacent space.

Janice's Space – Int. – Night

Smaller than the one preceding it, the room Janice occupies resembles a library or study, the walls are lined from floor to ceiling with bookshelves. In one corner is a large bed, in another a freestanding bathtub where Axel is busy taking a shower.

AXEL (*to Fred*)
There you are! Where were you? We were looking for you everywhere.

FRED
Twat!

Axel laughs.

The little girl pours some milk in a bowl for the monkey.

FRED
No, no milk. Especially not milk!

MANOU
Why not, does it give her a tummy ache?

FRED (*taking back the monkey*)
Yeah, tummy ache.
(*He goes up to Axel, looking determined*) Listen, there's something I have to tell you, I don't think you understand the situation.

Axel turns the showerhead on him, the jet of water hits him square in the face. Too enraged to care, the American whacks him on the back. Axel leaps out of the tub, howling in pain.

AXEL
Help! Janice, help!

Janice can't stop herself from laughing. Fred, embarrassed, recovers his poise. He takes off his soaked jacket and lets it fall to the ground.

FRED
Everybody just calm down, and you stop being a jackass.

Axel executes a somersault, landing in the bed sheets.

Fred, stunned, drops into an armchair. Manou picks up the jacket and places it delicately over a chair.

AXEL (*to Janice*)
You coming?

Janice looks at Fred, somewhat embarrassed by the journalist's presence.

(*to Fred*)
Listen padre, we'll talk about it tomorrow ok?

MANOU (*to Fred*)
Leave them alone, come with me.

Fred, with some reluctance, gets up and approaches the bed, just as Axel lifts the sheet and begins to furiously pedal his feet in the air, as though trying to ward off the blows of an adversary.

FRED
Watch out. Can't say I really give a shit, but if you go on acting like a jerk you're going to get burned.

He leaves, led by Manou who carries his jacket.

__Factory – Int. – Night__
We follow them down a long corridor opening onto a large room fitted out like a kitchen. Fred looks around, worried.

FRED
What's this?

MANOU
The kitchen stupid!

FRED
Whose kitchen?

MANOU
Everyone's.

FRED
Who's everyone? You mean it's like a commune?

MANOU
Well yes, actually no. It's like whatever. Robert wants it to be a commune but no one listens to him.

FRED
Who's Robert? Your daddy?

MANOU
Oh no... I don't have a daddy. I can do what I want.

They mount a metal staircase at the top of which is a trap door.

Fred helps Manou lift it to reveal a large room where a young elegantly dressed black guy, Steve, is fiddling with a game console.

He acknowledges Fred with a nod. Intrigued, the American does likewise.

FRED (*to Manou*)
He live here too?

MANOU
He works here but he doesn't sleep. It's Jennifer who brought him.

The room opens onto the terrace where sheets are drying, at the end of which is a laundry room...

Laundry Room – Int. – Night

Amid laundry baskets, boxes of washing powder and several large washing machines, we see a man laid out on a double mattress, his eyes wide open staring into space. Suddenly he shoots straight up, his back rigid as though he had only a single articulation at the hips.

ERIC (*pointing at Fred*)
Who is he?

MANOU
He's an American. We know him, he's got a monkey!

With the same movement he lies back down. Pointing a finger, Manou indicates the empty space next to Eric.

MANOU (*to Fred*)
You just have to lie down there.

She goes to look for a blanket in the laundry basket. Fred remains frozen to the spot as if in a daze, his arms dangling.

MANOU
Do I have to make your bed for you as well?

FRED
No, it's okay.

She leaves. Fred, resigned, takes his place on the mattress.

ERIC
Move over.

FRED
What?

ERIC
On that side. You're disturbing Francis and Dominique.

FRED
What? Where?

Fred, taken aback, shifts his body to leave a wide-open space between himself and Eric.

Lying back down, Eric stretches out his arm to activate a washing machine jammed up against the mattress. The metallic buckling and rattling seem to give him great waves of pleasure.

Janice's Space – Int. – Night

Axel, who is naked, lies on the bed with Janice, chatting.

JANICE
So you were in on this stunt from the beginning?

AXEL
Are you kidding! It was me who started this stunt, as you put it.

JANICE
But why did you want to fuck up the TV, the telephones, satellites?

AXEL
I didn't *want* anything. Besides what happens with communications isn't so important.

JANICE
What is?

AXEL
It's... I don't know, it's hard to say. You see it's this thing that can unleash an amazing force...

We see that Manou has come back into the room.

MANOU
Is it the Russians?

JANICE
It's none of your concern. Come on, back to bed!

Manou goes over to kiss them both goodnight.

MANOU
G'night Janice. G'night Mister!

She grabs hold of Axel's ears to get a closer look at his face.

AXEL
Ow! That hurts!

MANOU
All right. I'm going.

As soon as she's out the door, Axel leaps on top of Janice and begins caressing her frenetically. Janice undresses.

JANICE
But what is it exactly?

AXEL
Exactly what?

JANICE
This force!

He lets her go.

AXEL
It's like a cosmic energy... I mean, not exactly cosmic...

Excited, Janice straddles him.

Gradually, in a long cross-dissolve, an intermittent flicker of micro-cellular organisms begins to appear, superimposed on the scene of Axel and Janice making love. These fluorescent pulsings are of variable frequency and duration: three brief pulses followed by two longer ones, then five shorter ones, then nothing before the whole sequence repeats itself.

Chronobiology Lab – Int. – Day

Now completely visible, we see that the pulsings are being observed by Axel through an electron microscope. With his shoulders hunched over the apparatus, Axel is dressed in a white labcoat whose whiteness is made more dazzling by the neon striplights overhead.

The microscope is connected to an oscilloscope. An automated pen traces the rhythms of the waveforms on a roll of paper that cascades to the floor and mounts in a concertinaed pile. The micro-organisms seem to be emitting a form of morse code, an impression accentuated by Axel rhythmically tapping his fingers on the table as he watches.

Suddenly the door opens, causing a window to fly open violently. The wind tunnel lifts the length of paper from the floor, waving it like a pennant in the face of the new arrival, a guy in his thirties who is the director of the laboratory. Indifferent to the disturbances, Axel turns hastily towards him.

AXEL
We've got it ... take a look! I've found this regular micro-rhythm the chloroplasts are emitting. This is incredible. This is like fucking Nobel-Prize incredible. The discovery of the century! A language! I mean ... something like a language, that comes from the very depths of cellular life!

The director smiles, brushing away the printout with the back of his hand.

DIRECTOR
Can I ask our Nobel-in-waiting to shut the window?

Axel complies.

AXEL
Don't you see? The chloroplasts of this mutant strain of phyto-plankton are sending out messages. Wouldn't you agree?

DIRECTOR (*with a hint of irony*)
Of a sort. Hope you're writing it all down, their message to the world.

AXEL
Listen, this is serious. Anyway I've got an idea and you're going to help me. I want to expose the strain to the same series of light pulses and see if they respond and then if the response changes.

The puzzled face of the director.

AXEL
What's with you? Don't you think it's good manners to respond when something speaks to you?

Janice's Space – Int. – Night

JANICE
And so?

AXEL
And so what?

JANICE
And so what happened then? Tell me everything or I'll shop you to the feds!

Janice traps Axel in a headlock but he soon slips free. He jumps to a standing position, runs up against a wall and scales it to an impressive height before doing a back-flip and landing again on his feet.

AXEL (*as he lands*)
You have to catch me first. Okay, the director was a bit of an

asshole, but he was cool about it at least. He let me go on with the experiment. The problem was it didn't work so they fired me.

JANICE
No shit!

AXEL
In a way it was because I'd already decided to continue on my own. I realised I'd screwed up somehwere, that it didn't work with light waves, so I'd have to try something else. So I started again, this time using hertzian sound waves, I set up a small lab in the suburbs of Brussels, and that's when it started working.

JANICE
Sick! Hertzian waves. Frequency modulated?

AXEL
Natürlich.

JANICE
And did it get back to you?

AXEL
Not so fast... At first there was no clear response. But then I discovered that the chloroplasts of the phytoplankton were just a relay, it was a whole other deal.

JANICE
Wait a sec, chloroplasts, sorry to be remedial but what are they again?

AXEL
The seat of photosynthesis.

JANICE
Right! But what's it relaying?

AXEL
Ah if you only knew!

He jumps again and grabs hold of the doorframe, swinging back and forth by his fingertips. Janice stubs out her cigarette and embraces him, lifting herself off the ground. They begin to swing together.

AXEL
We're always wondering whether there might be life or intelligence on other planets, way up in the stars ... but we never ask ourselves about the infinitely small ... maybe it could come from there, from a universe that's even smaller than protons, electrons, quarks...

Janice bites Axel, making him let go.

JANICE
Great! Wonderful! But now the whole thing's fucked. Those government assholes had to ruin it! For once they had something really interesting in their laps and they screwed it up. Just because it was disturbing their crappy TV and radio schedules. What harm could it do to them? It was actually pretty good; made a change from the usual bullshit. If they didn't like it they could always go fuck themselves.

AXEL (*scratching his thigh*)
Yeah but they found it was interfering with communications, radar, laser guidance systems...

JANICE
You know what I say? Fuck them, that's what I say. Let them choke on their cornflakes. Retire to a padded cell. Buy a ticket

to euthanasia. Just as long as they leave us the fuck alone... If we don't even have the right to communicate with another universe!

Standing on his head, Axel begins to fall asleep. Janice shakes him. She points at the pendant that has fallen across his face.

JANICE
What's that? A school medal?

AXEL
No, don't touch.

Janice lunges, tries to take it off him. The chain breaks.

AXEL
What the bitch!

She opens the locket. It contains a phial, which she holds in the palm of her hand.

JANICE
Is this the strain of phytoplankton you were on about?

Axel nods.

JANICE
So we could reestablish contact with ... with...

Communal Kitchen – Int. – Day

A small group is huddled around the table. Robert, who feigns indifference towards what's going on, picks absentmindedly on a guitar and forces a wheezing two-note refrain from his harmonica. With him are Steve and Janice.

Manou arrives to find them deep in conversation.

STEVE (*to Janice*)
You saying this shit is smaller than quarks. Okay, that's cool. But how you figure a little-bitty particle smaller than a quark is gonna start blowing radio waves out its ass? That shit is too weird.

JANICE
Why don't you ask him yourself?
(*To Manou*) Where's Axel?

MANOU
I know where he is. I'll go and fetch him!

She leaves.

JANICE
Robert, would you mind not playing that guitar in lieu of me garrotting you with the D string?

ROBERT
Why shouldn't I play? Man's got a right to sing the blues, no?

JANICE
Forget the blues, this is serious business!

ROBERT
Well you know what, I think it's serious bullshit. All these stories, I smell a rat, I smell a fucking plague of rats. For a start there's your boyfriend, what about his buddy?

JANICE
He's not his buddy, he's an American journalist...

ROBERT
Journalist, cop, what's the differential? And then this quark business, we have to see...

STEVE (*forestalling Robert*)
You know what, wise old man of the mountain, I think you're right. What the fuck can a quark have to say to the comrades in the pen?

Everyone laughs except Robert, who doesn't appreciate the joke.

ROBERT
Okay, do what you want! But I think I have the right to speak, I mean I don't want to come off like some bastard landlord, but it was me who squatted this place, and it's me who has to fix everything. So we should at least discuss it!

Axel arrives carrying Manou piggyback.

ROBERT (*to Manou*)
You get down from there!

MANOU
I thought it was forbidden to forbid?

ROBERT
That's none of your business!

MANOU
You're just jealous!

STEVE (*to Axel*)
Something I can't figure out is how your Infra-quark Universe

can interfere with radio waves when, quantically speaking, they're from a whole other-ass dimension.

AXEL
Look, for the moment the idea of the Infra-quark Universe is just a hypothesis. The only thing I'm sure of right now is that the strain functions as some kind of relay.

Eric and Fred burst in. Eric carries the monkey on his shoulder. Fred doesn't look too good: unshaven and unkempt, he looks like he's had a rough night.

MANOU (*to Steve, indicating Fred*)
Do you think he's a fairy?

STEVE
Hush child!

FRED (*to Axel*)
Axel, can you come here?

ROBERT
You don't smell anything? There's a strange odour about, don't you find... Reminds me a bit of a pigsty.

MANOU
Is he a fairy or a fed, a pig or a poke?

FRED (*extremely irritated*)
Of course I'm a fed, can't you tell from the way I dress?

STEVE (*aside to Axel*)
So if I got this right, there must be some kind of subatomic relay?

Axel takes a sheet of paper and a pencil and begins drawing.

AXEL
Yes, the way I figure it, it must be here. But then it's even more complicated because look...

FRED (*to Axel*)
I said I needed to talk to you!

AXEL
Fuck off. Can't you see we're working?

FRED
What are you up to?

AXEL
If you must know, we've decided to go on with the experiments.

Eric leans over the plan Axel has been drawing. He looks very interested.

FRED
What experiments? Oh yeah, the global clusterfuck experiments. Haven't you had enough?

AXEL
What's it to you?

ROBERT
Great, why don't you just call a press conference? Perfect!

AXEL
Don't worry. It's cool. He's going to wrap it up, aren't you my

old poppet? Your scoop, wrap it up, roll it up and stick it up your culo. Am I wrong? You're finished, you know it, you're fucking toast!

Fred gives Axel the finger to let him know he has had enough of this subject.

FRED
Is there nothing to drink in this rathole?

MANOU
I can make you some coffee. With milk?

FRED
I said drink!

Sound of mopeds from outside. Fred rushes over to the window.

FRED
Who's that?

MANOU
Antoine and Michèle.

Factory – Ext. – Day

We see two teenagers on mopeds, panniers stuffed with schoolbooks and ring binders. Slaloming to avoid the objects strewn in their path they cross the two internal courtyards, then speed off down the hillside road.

Factory – Int. – Day

Axel climbs the metal staircase, opens the trap door and enters Steve's attic space. He sets about clearing away the clutter.

Cooperative Hangar – Int. – Day

An immense hangar piled up with crates and boxes, some of which lie half-opened, revealing contents that include computer terminals, keyboards, video monitors, cables, tinned foods etc. Mr. Kao Ky, impeccably dressed in an old-style tunic, sits on an electric car that also serves as a mobile office, complete with desk and computer.

Another Asian man, the frail and wan-complexioned Mr. Wang, circulates on a forklift looking for materials that Kao Ky requests by barking into a microphone. Janice and Steve stand closeby. Janice studies a list while Steve checks the contents of a mounting stack of crates.

JANICE
Fibre optic cable LM 20.342.

KAO KY
Kao Ky he has that.
(*Speaking into the microphone*) Hello, Mr. Wang, LM 20.342!

Kao Ky follows Wang's movements on a video monitor.

KAO KY
No, not there. Farther. More to right, yes that way. Is good. See Kao Ky has that stuff.

STEVE
And what about a pediascope? Quadrichrome. An old one will do, even without software.

KAO KY
How you call? Quadrichrome pediascope. Yes Kao Ky has that too. Hello Mr. Wang! Aeroflot pediascope. You find in reserve zone. Next to tin food.

Suddenly Kao Ky notices the figure of Eric on his screen, scaling the shelves.

KAO KY
What he doing you friend? No meddle with merchandise.

Janice leans in to take a look at the screen.

KAO KY
What he want up there. What he trying to do?

JANICE (*speaking into the microphone*)
Hey Eric? Get down from there, come back here!

Eric ignores her completely.

JANICE
Oh let him be, he's harmless.

KAO KY
But is not stable. Is not stable you friend!

MR. WANG
Don't find Aeroflot pediascope, Mr. Ky.

KAO KY
Kao Ky know well he has pediascope. Kao Ky, he find.

(*To Janice, pointing at Eric*) Tell you friend not to steal, that stuff too expensive.

Kao Ky sets off. Steve steps onto the running board.

MR. WANG
It's okay. Wang find pediascope.

Kao Ky slams on the brakes, almost throwing Steve off the vehicle.

KAO KY
You pay tension. You friend, where is he you friend?

STEVE
Hold up a sec! What we gonna do about the serial numbers and registration?

KAO KY
No problem for serial numbers. Kao Ky he take care of that.

He calls Mr. Wang

KAO KY
Bring machine to make serial numbers. Yes you know well. Regional Bureau...

STEVE
Hey. None of this gets out. Keep it in the ground, you feel me?

KAO KY
But yes of course. No problem. Never problem with Kao Ky.

Cooperative Hangar – Ext. – Day

Steve and Janice begin loading the crates into the back of the van, while Eric, brandishing a retractable ruler like a sword, takes meaningless measurements all around the vehicle. Kao Ky observes them from his office window.

Street – Ext. – Day

The van is so weighed down that the chassis almost skims the road. In the back, Eric is literally walled in by crates, his body happily contorted.

On the sidewalk, we see a group of teenagers, among whom are Antoine and Michèle.

Suddenly, Michèle alerts Antoine to a flyer she has spotted, freshly plastered to the wall: a wanted notice offering a reward for the capture of Axel and Fred.

MICHÈLE (*to Antoine*)
Look!

ANTOINE
40,000!

Approaching the flyer, they are suddenly accosted by a man in a gabardine raincoat.

MAN
Interest you does it? Perhaps you know something about it.

MICHÈLE
No, I'm afraid ... but if we did you can be sure that...

Factory – Int. – Day

Fred inspects the building with its odd mix of furnished rooms and ruined, abandoned spaces.

He pushes aside a heavy curtain and discovers a room decked out in elegant bourgeois style complete with night tables, wall lamps and matching rugs.

On one side is Antoine and Michèle's desk, together with two tables piled up with schoolbooks.

Continuing his explorations he arrives at an almost empty room, beautiful in its Japanese-style minimalism.

FEMALE VOICE
Shoes!

Fred retreats to the doorway, takes off his shoes and then pads back into the room. We see a young redhaired woman in her thirties, Jennifer, kneeling before an engraving.

JENNIFER (*with extreme concentration*)
The kite
In the same place
As the sky yesterday

She ignores Fred as he crosses the room, exits through another door and continues on until he reaches the kitchen.

Kitchen – Int. – Day

Manou, her sleeves rolled up to her elbows, slaps a large lump of dough on the table. Startled by the noise, the monkey takes refuge on top of the fridge.

MANOU
So who is it you like best?

FRED
Who what?

MANOU
Eric or Axel?

FRED (*flustered*)
It's the same.

MANOU
So you're jealous then?

FRED
Jealous? Of what?

MANOU
Of Axel making *jing-jing* with Janice?

Enraged, Fred grabs the ball of dough and raises his arm as though to fling it in the little girl's face. Engine sounds.

MANOU
They're back!

She wipes her hands on her sweatshirt and skips out the door. The camera follows.

<u>Factory – Ext. – Day</u>

Manou goes to open the rear doors of the van. Eric's body is "stacked" among the crates. Steve sounds the car horn. Axel arrives on the scene. Robert pokes his head out the window.

ROBERT
Quiet, I'm trying to compose!

Jennifer appears at another window.

JENNIFER
Robert. Stop yelling.

AXEL (*to Janice*)
Did you get everything?

JANICE
Pretty much. The essentials anyway.

Axel grabs her by the neck to kiss her. She pushes him away and turns to pick up a crate.

STEVE (*to Axel*)
That's the way she is, just gotta groove with it. You gonna give me a hand unloading this shit?

With a resigned sigh, Axel picks up a crate and carries it to Steve's space. Fred appears at the foot of the stairs.

FRED (*to Axel*)
Wait, let me help you with that.

AXEL
What's with you? Miss your deadline?

FRED
Something like that. So anyway, what have I got to lose?

AXEL
Sure, here, take it from this end.

Fred passes his monkey to Eric who cradles it in his arms like a baby. Up in the "laboratory," Axel sets down the crate and gives instructions how to install the various devices. A febrile atmosphere takes hold as he grabs a piece of chalk and draws the assembly diagram on the wall.

AXEL
The sequences will be coded with this device.

FRED
What do you mean by sequences?

AXEL
Oh it's just a phase really, it doesn't necessarily mean anything on its own. But then the coded sequences are transmitted by this machine here in the form of hertzian waves.

FRED
The same setup you had in Belgium?

JANICE (*aggressively*)
Oh so you're interested now?

STEVE
What's going on? You planning on continuing with that reportage of yours?

FRED (*with a shrug*)
No … but maybe one day I'll write a book about all this.

MANOU (*to Axel*)
Yes, but in Brussels you got caught and they blew everything up and if Fred hadn't arrived you would have been blown to little pieces and they'd have to scrape you off the walls.

JANICE (*calling Axel to account*)
So you're sure we won't be discovered. Cause even if the radio wave disturbances start again, with that thing there (she indicates a half-opened mini-radar dish) they won't be able to figure out our position.

Robert's head appears through the trap door. He carries a huge basket of laundry under one arm. He begins to ferret around in the room.

ROBERT
How's it going with your UIQ?

MANOU
You say "You I Cue!"

ROBERT
You I who?

Fred writes it in chalk on the wall.

FRED
You I Cue. Universe of the Infra-Quark.

ROBERT
What the fuck is he still doing here?

FRED
Bother you some?

115

ROBERT
Yeah, as a matter of fact. This is my place!

Eric steps between them, bearing his teeth at Robert like the monkey.

ROBERT (*disconcerted*)
Calm down, Eric, it's okay!

Michèle and Antoine appear, both carrying ring binders.

MICHÈLE
What's going on here?

Antoine elbows her, having immediately recognized Axel and Fred. Michèle too recognizes the wanted men. Excited, and with a conspiratorial air, they signal to Robert who takes no notice.

MANOU (*to Robert*)
Haven't you got something better to do, like the laundry?

ROBERT (*leaving the room*)
Cheeky little shit! I'm telling you it'll end in tears.

Michèle and Antoine follow him out of the room.

Factory Terrace – Ext. – Day
Antoine unfolds the poster he has ripped from the wall .

ANTOINE
You see that? (*he points at the two photos of Axel and Fred*)
And that? (*he indicates the reward*) 40,000 is no small change!

ROBERT
You see this, you little fuckwit!

He slaps him around the head.

ROBERT
Do I make myself clear?

ANTOINE (*pitifully*)
Hey, take it easy, Robert. I was just kidding.

<u>Lab – Int. – Night</u>

All the connections have been made, numerous cables snake across the floor.

AXEL (*to Janice*)
Ok, it's all yours.

Fred, Manou, Steve and Jennifer turn towards her as she takes out the phial she removed from Axel's pendant, breaks it open and pours the solution onto a glass slide. There is a general holding of breath as she carefully covers it with another slide and then slips it under the lens of the electron microscope, which is connected to a screen. Axel switches it on and we see a high definition image of the cellular organisms pulsing with an irregular glow.

JANICE
What's going on? You think it's normal for it to be flashing so randomly?

AXEL
Yes, I think so.

He adjusts the image on the electronic oscilloscope where we see a horizontal line tracing out the pulse variations. Steve is sitting in front of the sequence generator: a keyboard that triggers hertzian waves, which it sends over to the phytoplankton sample.

STEVE
Let's party.

AXEL
Ok... Go!

Steve taps out a "phrase," similar to a message in Morse code. No apparent change is noted on the electronic oscilloscope.

MANOU
What's he up to Mr. UIQ? Is he sleeping? Why doesn't he answer?

JANICE
Maybe he's gone for a stroll in another galaxy.

MANOU
No, no … it's not like that, he has to come back!

Try again, Steve!

Steve tries again with another sequence and then several more but there is still no response. Everyone becomes despondent.

JENNIFER
It doesn't look like it wants to answer...

STEVE
I'm smoked. I'm gonna catch some Z's.

MANOU
Move over, out of the way. Let me do it!

She lunges at the table and trips over a cable causing the sequence generator to fall.

STEVE (*furious*)
Manou, beat it!

MANOU
I'm sick of this. It's not my fault if your stupid machine doesn't work.

JANICE
To bed, now!

She opens the trap door and ushers Manou out.

Axel gathers up the machine, takes off the hood and examines the damage.

AXEL
It's nothing.
(*To Steve*) You got any microwelding gear around here?

Steve rummages in a crate and hands him a welding gun.

STEVE
This do?

AXEL
Perfect.

JANICE
You gonna do that now?

AXEL
Why not?

JANICE
Well, I have to go, I'm late.

STEVE
I'll come with you. I have to take back Doom Nation V.

He indicates a discarded console game in the corner.

AXEL (*to Janice*)
You ditching me girl? Say it isn't so.

JANICE (*laughing*)
Yeah, you're a fucking drag.

Steve moves away, Janice grabs him by the arm. Axel watches as they leave together.

Steve's Car – Ext. / Int. – Night

The car zips down several streets. Janice and Steve are talking. Both look worried.

JANICE
What do you think? Is it going to work?

STEVE
I don't know jack shit. What about you?

JANICE
Well there's no reason…

STEVE
But I can see this turning into a situation.

JANICE
Meaning?

STEVE
A warrant for Axel and Fred.

JANICE
Come off it. They dish out more warrants than parking tickets.

The car parks in front of the video store and Steve pops his game into the returns box.

<u>Laundry – Int. – Night</u>

Fred, his monkey and Eric are asleep. Suddenly Eric jackknifes up, his back stiff as a board, and sets the washing machine in motion. Fred awakens with a violent start.

FRED
Hey! Turn that machine off.

ERIC
What machine?

FRED
The wa-shing-ma-chine! That thing, there!

ERIC
Impossible.

FRED
Why impossible? Just press the stop button.

ERIC
Impossible because if I stop it the Earth stops. And secondly, if it starts up again, it's going to turn in the opposite direction. In which case we will be in a well of woe and lamentation. Thirdly, it's none of your fucking business. Fourthly, Francis and Dominique wouldn't like it. And fifthly, because it does something to me...

FRED
And what might that be?

Eric gives him the finger, Fred shrugs his shoulders.

ERIC (*politely*)
You'll just have to get used to it.

FRED
Fine!

He wraps himself in a blanket and goes out onto the terrace.

<u>Terrace – Ext. – Night</u>

The moon illumines the factory and surrounding buildings, bathing them in an air of mystery. Fred lights a cigarette, his shadow plays across the hanging sheets. Hearing noises coming from the laboratory, he goes over to the door to see what's going on.

Lab – Int. – Night

Now alone in the lab room, Axel taps out sequences on the repaired generator. After a short delay, the sequence is approximately reproduced on the oscilloscope.

FRED
It's working.

AXEL
Yes, I think it's responding. I'm going to get Janice. You take over.

FRED (*intimidated*)
No, I don't think I'm able.

AXEL
Don't be stupid, try...

As Fred sits down at the console, Axel picks up a telephone directory.

Before he has time to consult it, the phone rings. He picks up.

AXEL
Hello ... what? Who is this?

Robert and Manou's Space – Int. – Night

Little Manou holds the receiver.

MANOU
I'm telling you ... there's something in the TV.

Robert bangs on the TV set, the image is all disrupted.

MANOU (*to Robert*)
Stop, you're going to break it...

MANOU (*to Axel*)
Axel, you have to come, he's going to break the TV!

The sound comes back, an Eastern European sports commentary. Then the war film they had been watching comes back on with an unrelated sound now accompanying the images.

Suddenly, in a kind of media cataclysm, we see a rapid succession of random images from channels all over the world, frequently superimposed and with the sounds all jumbled up in a grotesque cacophony.

ROBERT
If I'm not wrong, it's starting again, isn't it?

Lab – Int. – Night

Fred, Robert, Manou, Michèle and Antoine are gathered around Axel who operates the signal transmitter. They all notice, with varying degrees of interest, that something finally appears to be happening. Janice storms in with Steve.

JANICE
So it is true, it responds!

AXEL
Look...

Axel taps out a sequence for the bacteria sample. After a long moment of silence, blobs of fluorescent light begin to rearrange themselves on the main screen of the electronic microscope.

124

The oscilloscope shows a succession of peaks and flat lines corresponding to the short sounds emitted by Axel.

JANICE
Can I try?

AXEL
Sure, go ahead!

Janice taps a slightly more elaborate sequence. UIQ tries to reproduce it, fails, tries again but can't manage.

MANOU (*speaking towards the sample*)
No, that's not it, pay attention ... it's not like that!

Janice plays the same sequence again.

After a moment's hesitation, UIQ manages to reproduce the message correctly. Everyone seems fascinated, except Robert who remains studiously indifferent.

ROBERT
Very clever, but your wotsitsname is still fucking up the TV!
A man can't even watch a film in peace...

AXEL
I think it's when he doesn't get it straight away that he loses the plot. But it doesn't matter, it's just a phase.

JENNIFER
Maybe, but it scares people, you know...

AXEL
Who cares? I'm telling you, it's just a phase, we'll sort it out.

We just have to wait until we've fixed things ... so they can't trace us.

ANTOINE (*looking scornfully at them all, somewhat pompous*)
Who cares? Who cares? Perhaps we ought to discuss it. So this is your idea of fun, is it? Screwing up emergency services, satellite links?

MICHÈLE (*haughty*)
Oh, let them play with their toys!

JANICE
Shut up you two. I can't hear anything.

She plays a simple sequence which UIQ repeats. Slowly at first, and then more and more frenetically.

MANOU (*to UIQ*)
Good, that's very good!

Manou pushes Janice aside.

MANOU
Now it's my turn. It's my turn!

She taps out an extremely complicated sequence, which UIQ tries and fails to copy.

AXEL
That's too difficult.

MANOU
Okay, let me try something else...

She taps out another sequence which she hums along to. UIQ tries to repeat it. She plays another long sequence, which UIQ gets in a muddle.

Taxi – Ext./Int. – Night

A driver sits at the wheel of his car, parked in a taxi rank. A familiar signal tells him he has a call. He lifts the receiver. Off-screen we hear a loud and brutal cacophony of voices. The driver jumps back with a start.

DRIVER
This is the Taxi!

The noise becomes unbearable.

Lights go on suddenly, windows open.

Terrified, the driver gets out and runs away.

Lab – Int. – Night

On the oscilloscope the waveform's peaks and troughs become extremely chaotic, breaking into dots, lines and stochastic patterns.

Michèle and Antoine are no longer present.

JANICE
Manou, you can't just do any old thing with that.

ROBERT
When are you lot going to stop with your psychotic squiggling?

Appalled, the others turn towards him.

ROBERT (*lowering his tone*)
I mean can't I just see my bloody programme!

Axel contemplates the screen.

AXEL
Let her do it, watch!

Eric begins to dance making odd, jerky movements.

JENNIFER
It's incomprehensible... But I ask myself if UIQ might not have some kind of rapport with what the Hindus call *bhaktevadanta swami prabhypaba*?

STEVE (*ironically*)
Ah yes, the famous nectar of the gods. You are surely right sister. I don't see any other possible explanation.

Suddenly, on a larger screen, geodesic measurements appear, together with a moving dot.

JANICE
Manou, I forbid you to type in whatever you feel like. That machine is not for kids.

MANOU
He can't repeat things, but it's cute what he does, don't you think?

Eric dances with increasing savagery, throwing himself against Robert, headbutting him in the chest.

ROBERT
You're all fucking crazy. He was never this bad. I'm telling

you, we should throw all this shit out, get rid of it. It must be something cooked up by the Americans, or the Russians ... it could be some kind of biological weapon for all we know!

The screen flashes on again with its geodesic measurements. Then, suddenly, we see a pair of hands approaching...

<u>Control Tower – Int. – Day</u>

...the hands of an air-traffic controller.

In the room the atmosphere is tense.

With an index finger, the controller follows the trajectory of the moving dot.

CONTROLLER
He's ignoring all instructions, what the hell is he doing ... with 300 passengers aboard!

SECOND CONTROLLER
Resume contact immediately. Emergency Program 1.

<u>Boeing – Int. – day</u>

The anguished face of a male passenger, one hand over his rapidly pumping heart.

<u>Control Tower – Int. – day</u>

The controller switches on a microphone.

CONTROLLER
This is control. Order to correct your flight path immediately.

Do you hear me? Correct your flight path, for chrissakes. Immediate correction. Emergency. Get back up in the air...

Boeing – Int. – Day

The same worried passenger unbuckles his seatbelt and gets down on all fours in the gangway. Tossed by the jolting plane, he appears to be trying to retrieve a fallen pen. The pen rolls under the feet of a woman passenger. The guy crawls over to her and leaps at her throat.

MALE PASSENGER
My pen, give me back my pen, bitch!

The woman smashes him on the head. He crumples to the ground, stunned by the blow.

We see the legs of the hostess passing rapidly down the corridor until she reaches the cockpit. She is hardly in the door when the pilot and co-pilot turn towards her, looking dismayed. Confused, she examines her uniform.

VOICE-OFF
This is Control...

A cacophony of voices gradually resolves into a mass bleating of goats.

Beach – Ext. – Day

On the beach of a Club Med are numerous sunbathers, many with transistor radios. A small boy plays with a paper airplane, making engine sounds with his mouth.

Overhead, an ultralight aircraft appears. The pilot waves to the boy who launches his plane in the man's direction...

Suddenly, we hear a terrifying screaming noise as the upside down Boeing appears out of nowhere, skimming the ground, its tail drawing a line in the sand. It passes just beneath the ultralight, thrusting it up into the sky at great speed...

The wind from the plane's jetstream sweeps everything away from the beach: sun umbrellas, beach cabins, trees, everything is turned upside down.

People are buried up to their necks in sand.

BOY
Mummy, where's my plane?

MOTHER
Hey, let's just see if we can find daddy first, then we'll look for your plane.

The Boeing does a loop the loop and passes over again, throwing up enormous waves of sand. Radios lie scattered in all directions, emitting a strange music of whale song and bleating goats.

Boeing – Int./Ext. – Day

The horrified head of a woman passenger with her hair sticking straight up, nose pressed against the window.

Outside, in what looks like a corolla, a man appears to shoot up feet first... It's the ultralight pilot with his parachute.

Back in the Boeing, the passenger is belted into her seat, the plane upside down with all loose items (hand baggage, trolleys, trays, bottles etc.) now on the ceiling.

Beach – Ext. – Day

The wings of the ultralight crumple onto the sand, as the parachutist descends.

PARACHUTIST (*to the people down below*)
Look out! Get out of the way!

Animal music in the radios.

GUY ON BEACH
What is this shit? That's it. This time they've really jumped the shark.

He kicks a radio.

BOY
Where's my plane? Has anybody seen my plane?

City – Ext. – Day

A limousine rolls down a wide avenue.

In the back seat, the President of the Investigation Commission into Hertzian Disturbances discusses the matter with the commission spokesman.

SPOKESMAN (*a sandwich in his hand*)
Mr. President, do you really think we can let things go on like this?

PRESIDENT
I don't see why not ... as long as we downplay it.

SPOKESMAN
Downplay it, very well Mr. President. Pointless, then, to insist on what happened at Sarrebrück, Agadir, Kingston...

PRESIDENT (*nodding*)
Hmm, quite pointless...

The car stops at the foot of a glass office tower. The two men get out and head towards the entrance with its military guards.

PRESIDENT
Agadir?

SPOKESMAN
Yes Mr. President, the air disaster...

PRESIDENT
But there were no victims!

SPOKESMAN
No, no victims to speak of.

PRESIDENT
So we can forget about it, just let it drift on its silent wings far from the public's mind, especially as there haven't been any other incidents since, of any note. Have there?

SPOKESMAN
Well, one member of the Commission has raised an objection regarding the F.A.H.

PRESIDENT
Refer him to the relevant technical sub-committee...

Factory – Int. – day

The tramp Fred encountered the night he arrived stands at the foot of the building in the second courtyard. He furrows his brow, perplexed by what he sees. Myriad bunches of cable cascade from the upper floor where the laboratory is installed to enter other rooms below. It looks as if the facade is in the grip of a giant octopus...

Manou appears at the kitchen window. The tramp hides behind a wall.

Kitchen – Int. – Day

Manou, still at the window, addresses someone off-screen.

MANOU
I just saw someone.

VOICE-OFF (*bizarre-sounding*)
Who was it?

An intricate system of machines occupies the room. The voice appears to be coming from a screen, on which we can distinguish traits suggesting a face.

MANOU
Someone we don't know, but I know him, because sometimes I see him when I go to my special cave.

UIQ
Your case?

MANOU
No! My *cave*! Never mind, it's too complicated. I'll explain it to you another time... Let's get back to work.

134

The face decomposes. In its place a schematic three-dimensional hand appears, with rings containing microchips on all six fingers.

MANOU
No I don't want it like that!

UIQ
Why not? It's good like that!

MANOU
No, I told you it's not like that. There are too many fingers for a start!

The image immediately corrects itself.

UIQ
Oh, sorry. My mistake. None...the...less... You did tell me I forget, that you have only five fingers at present.

MANOU
Why? Was it different before?

UIQ
Yes! And so it will be again!

MANOU
Ah, yes! Of course, when we were all centipedes? Anyway, what do we do now?

A list of materials scrolls down the screen.

UIQ
We have to assemble all this, and in order. You'll see, it will be easy as pie in the sky.

MANOU
Oh noooh! I'll never be able to do all that. Wait, I'll get Fred. You stay here, okay?

She takes off in the direction of Janice's space.

Corridor – Int. – Day

Manou tramples over the cables that have by now completely invaded the corridors and interior spaces. She bursts into Janice's room.

Janice's Space – Int. – Day

In Janice's room, another workstation has been set up, huddled around which we now find Steve, Axel and Fred. They watch as complex graphs and mathematical formulae continue to flash across the screen.

MANOU
Fred, you have to come right away.

FRED
What is it now?

MANOU
You have to help me. I don't understand anything.

Fred sighs.

MANOU
Come on, it's for the work UIQ and I are doing.

FRED
What work?

MANOU
To make a machine that fires bullets. Well, of course they're not *real* bullets... Because only *I* can see them. But people will feel them when they get hit. Come on. It'll be great. It's an idea I had. It's really brilliant. UIQ thinks so too and he's going to do everything to see that it works. The only thing is he doesn't have hands or feet or a nose, or anything at all in fact. So you have to come to help us with the welding and stuff.

Manou drags Fred out of the room.

Axel and Steve seem unconcerned by the equations that now fill the screen.

STEVE (*to the screen*)
What you're saying seems a million miles from our current cosmological theories...

AXEL
... which are nonetheless based on pretty much irrefutable experimental evidence!

The blurred face of UIQ, consisting of little more than the three black holes of the eyes and mouth, appears on the screen.

UIQ
I am not contesting your experimental methods ... the problem is your obsession with what you call the Big Bang theory ... you cannot seem to escape it but it is a road to nowhere being that the starting point is completely erroneous.

STEVE
How so?

UIQ
The expansion of the universe so called.

AXEL
And the Doppler-Fizeau effect?

UIQ
An illusion resulting from your anthropological perspective, which is to say dependent on co-ordinates proper to beings limited, discreet, defined, finite in space and time, according to linear, irreversible sequences. Ours is another approach to the cosmos, there being no reason to think in terms of a before and after your so-called Big Bang. If such a thing exists, then it must be happening everywhere and at every instant. Is it clear enough? But let us by all means return to a physical mathematical model.

The face disappears, once again replaced by mathematical formulae. Suddenly we hear a series of cries, like the wails of a newborn infant. Axel and Steve sigh in unison.

Michèle and Antoine's Space – Int. – Day
The screams startle the two high school students as they enjoy an intimate lunch together. They both look incensed.

STEVE
Not that again!

AXEL
I'll go and see what's happening.

STEVE (*to the screen*)
How is it a universe like you can be so cool with us and at the same time such a dumb-ass with her?

UIQ
Steve, you know I like you a lot, but you can be a real nunce sometimes. To be dumb-ass or not to be dumb-ass, that is the question ... that was posed on the road to dumb-asscus...

The camera follows Axel to the laboratory.

Lab – Int. – Day

Much has changed in the lab where a mess of cables run in all directions and a great disorder reigns.

Janice, her skull covered in electrodes connected to a new machine, works with a welding gun on an integrated circuit.

Noticeably thinner and looking exhausted, she speaks to the oscilloscope screen where the face of UIQ is visible...

JANICE
Easy, we'll get there...

UIQ (*whining*)
Aah, Eee, Oooh, Vvv — Yeeeooooh, Aah, Eee, Vvv — Eee, Oooh, Aaaah, Vvv...

JANICE
Sshh, quietly now... It's okay, don't worry, I'm here.

UIQ continues whining.

The sound is suddenly transformed into a piercing animal cry akin to whale song. The face becomes deformed, its traits begin to fluctuate.

JANICE
No, don't start that again, or I'll stop right now, I'll pull your plug!

UIQ recommences its infant wailing, sending Janice into a violent, uncontrollable spasm. Axel rushes towards her, she looks deathly pale. As he removes one of the electrodes from her forehead, she jumps up.

JANICE
Don't fucking touch that!

Axel backs off.

AXEL
What the hell is wrong with you?

JANICE
What's wrong? I'll tell you what's wrong. You're never there when you're supposed to be, I have to do everything. I've had enough, he's driving me up the fucking wall. And it's all your fault he's like that!

AXEL
My fault?

JANICE
Yes, what he needs ... is a real male imago!

AXEL
A male what? What the fuck's an imago?

JANICE
Forget it, forget it, your head's bypassed the event horizon of your ass. Oh, it's easy playing equations all day when I have to teach him his fucking ABCs and dry his liquid crystal tears!

AXEL
Look, get some rest. I'll take over if you want.

JANICE
No way. You don't know how to deal with him. I can just see it, you'll just get him on some fucking catastrophe theory trip and I'll come back and find him even more upset than when I left!

AXEL
Okay, okay. Have it your way. I'm not going to say another word.

Axel hoists himself up onto a bar overhead and hangs upside down.

UIQ stops crying and begins speaking again in a detached tone.

UIQ
I'm not going to say another word, I'm not going to say another word.

International Commission Headquarters – Int. – Day

The face of a nervous-looking man appears in extreme close-up, scrutinizing a TV screen where we see two superimposed images: a gyrating stripper and the blurred and enigmatic face of UIQ.

A subtitle reads: "We apologise for these disturbances which are beyond our control."

He switches channel. The face is still there.

He inserts a tape into the VCR and presses record.

MALE VOICE-OFF
Play that back.

We are in a large glass-walled room where around thirty technicians, engineers, researchers and military staff are busy at their different workstations amid a febrile ambience of voices, telephone call signals, etc. In one corner a group of statisticians are in discussion in front of a giant electronic world map on which three particular territories appear highlighted in different colours.

PRESIDENT
Ireland, maybe that can offer us a lead.

STATISTICIAN
Yes, but what about Uganda?

OTHER MAN
And Quebec? I don't see the connection.

PRESIDENT
There must be a solution, we just have to find it. Why is it that, out of all the world's nations, these three countries have been spared the disturbances? There must be some kind of logical explanation...

STATISTICIAN (*aside*)
Yeah, right!

Near them, a military officer is on the phone trying to hear what is being said to him.

OFFICER
Quiet, it's NATO high command... They're asking if the Russians have been affected.

TECHNICIAN
Affected by what?

OFFICER
Well, stuff like that (*he indicates the blurred face on the video image*).

STATISTICIAN
They probably know more than us about it, the commie faggots.

OFFICER
They're saying the Russians think they may have experienced something of the kind, but they're not sure, they want us to verify.

STATISTICIAN
Why don't they fuck off back to Siberia.

On the other side of the glass panel, the spokesman for the International Commission is giving a press conference.

JOURNALIST
You've kept us hanging around here for six hours. So what is it? What the fuck is going on? Can't you try to be a little more precise?

SPOKESMAN
All I can say at the present time is that we have the situation well in hand. The disturbances are now completely under control. As you can see, air traffic is back to operating normally and

all radio communications have been re-established. Including with the countries of the Eastern Bloc.

One journalist indicates a TV screen where the blurred face is plainly visible.

JOURNALIST
And what are you planning to do about Mr. Smiley there?

SPOKESMAN
There are of course still a few residual traces!

JOURNALIST
Call that a residual trace?

SPOKESMAN
It's a completely harmless phenomenon, clearly an F.A.H. effect: a Floating Anthropomorphic Halo.

ANOTHER JOURNALIST
About which you clearly know S.F.A.

SPOKESMAN
I must ask you to moderate your language, sir. While I understand your sentiments I must remind you that I represent the International Commission which the Security Council has charged by to investigate the phenomena of which we speak.

Manou & Robert's Space – Int. – Day

Manou lies in the hammock making rhythmic movements with her hand, which has odd-looking rings on all the fingers.

We hear an electric buzzing sound punctuated by short high-pitched tones: she is playing with a kind of ball that appears in the form of a red halo that she directs remotely to strike different objects. The ball ricochets off a wall and hits Robert who jumps back as though from an electric shock.

ROBERT
Ouch!

(He leaps up at one stroke). That's it! Give me that thing. Now! We told you not to play with it.

MANOU (*with sweet insincerity*)
Sorry... I didn't mean to hit you!

ROBERT
That hurt. You want me to do it to you?

Manou shrugs and goes on with her game. Fred's monkey has taken cover on top of a wardrobe. From the corner of her eye, Manou checks to make sure Robert isn't looking before targeting the animal with the ball. Strident squeals are heard as the monkey runs off. Robert turns once again menacingly towards the little girl.

MANOU (*playing innocent*)
What's up with her?

Factory – Ext. – Day

Jumping down from the hammock, she pursues the animal outside across the two inner courtyards. After being hit several times, the monkey disappears into the dark of a hangar. Manou goes looking for it and runs into the tramp. Terrified, she freezes. Both of them look each other up and down. Manou involuntarily directs the ball at the tramp, hitting him square in the face. He howls in pain before straightening up to protect himself, whipping out a knife whose blade flashes in the darkness. Manou runs away as fast as her legs can carry her.

We see Manou, pursued by the monkey who gnashes her teeth.

Out in the yard, she trips and falls head first into a dark puddle. She gets up, wrings out her skirt and sees Eric sitting on the edge of the puddle, methodically stripping away an old crate. With his teeth he cuts the wood into sticks of different lengths that he then measures in a kind of ritual.

MANOU
What are you doing?

Eric doesn't answer. Manou takes off her "rings" and slips them inside her pocket to watch Eric. The red halo disappears.

The schizo meticulously selects a small piece of wood, which he throws into the water, aiming at a precise spot on the surface. He does the same with a second piece. Manou gathers up a handful of sticks that she throws in at random. Surprise! The pieces form themselves into a face.

Manou stops to contemplate the face for an instant, then picks up a baton and agitates the water with it, making it look as though the face is laughing.

Eric gathers up the metallic pastilles that he had placed around the puddle. The face decomposes, slipping piece by piece beneath the water.

We hear a moaning sound coming from the laboratory. Manou raises her eyes towards the upper floor of the building.

146

Lab – Int. – Day

No longer wearing electrodes, Janice approaches the screen where UIQ's face is visible.

JANICE
What's wrong?

The closer she gets, the more the face of UIQ appears to diminish in size. When she is sitting next to him, they are the same size, and he's partly masked by her head.

JANICE
I don't know whether you're really confused or you're just jerking me around. I've already explained to you a hundred times the notion of the sexuated individual.

UIQ
Yes, tell me about that... Oh please, tell me again.

JANICE
I'm getting a bit tired of repeating myself.

UIQ
You don't want to talk to me anymore, is that it?

JANICE
No, but … look, let's take it from the beginning, most living things are created from the conjunction of two types of beings that are at once similar and different, a father and a mother, but it's not always the case.

As UIQ speaks, we pass to Michèle and Antoine's room. Antoine is lying down on his stomach. Michèle leans over his naked torso,

147

squeezing blackheads and spots, several of which ooze inordinate quantities of pus. Antoine grimaces with pain, trying not to cry out.

UIQ (*off*)
Yes, snails I understand. Therefore it's only when there is, as you say, sexuated reproduction. So, what does this difference in sexes consist of? Does it only concern the enchaining of DNA and RNA sequences in the genetic encoding? And if that's the case, how does one explain the need for the phases of development and learning? So many questions... Does the distinction between two beings always have a genetic base? Do they need to be co-present? The phenomena of interaction seem to suggest as much... And yet is this still true when the two beings are billions and billions of light years apart, or when they belong to incomparable systems of coordinates? As it is between your system and ours.

JANICE
You just said it, "your system and ours." You see, you understand perfectly well the distinction between two beings.

UIQ
Yours, mine, ours. You, me, you, me. *You* ... yes I understand you. But *me*... Me, I'll never get it. This face on the screen is only for you. And if you want that I ... that I change it...

UIQ's face metamorphoses, its traits become deformed, passing through a series of changes to end up in the shape of a grotesque mask though the two eyes and mouth subsist.

UIQ
Do you like me like this?

JANICE
Not really... I preferred the way you were before...

UIQ
As you wish!

UIQ returns to the previous image.

UIQ
But let us stick to our knitting... I'm sorry, but I think we have to go back to a higher level, to the opposition between here and there... You didn't give me an answer. Is there always a sexual opposition? You see, in what you call my Infra-quark Universe, there is no axiomatic system establishing polar distinctions of the type you-me. There, if I ... if I ... may say so, beings delimit themselves without limiting each other. From this it might be possible to proceed in two directions: your fuzzy logic, but it seems a bit vague, a bit embryonic ... or another, more promising logic I would say, that of poetry...

<u>Park – Ext. – Day</u>

At the foot of a monumental stairway, lined with statues. Laden with a big cardboard box, Eric throws handfuls of grain towards the pigeons which flock around him to the point that he becomes almost invisible under a cloud of beating wings. Not far from him Manou, wearing a microphone-equipped headset, is in conversation with UIQ. She circles around Eric, placing little metallic pastilles on the ground.

MANOU
Is that it? Enough? More? Don't you think you're overdoing it? There won't be any left for tomorrow.

Suddenly a vehement speech resounds through the park. On the esplanade, at the top of the steps, a hysterical preacher standing on a wooden box harangues a growing, anxious crowd of onlookers. He holds up a large banner on which we recognize UIQ's blurred face.

PREACHER

In truth it was all written. Beware!

(*He points at a woman*) Beware sinner! Have you no shame! I speak the truth. Only he who submits will be spared the final punishment!

SOMEONE IN THE CROWD

What submission?

PREACHER (*brandishing his banner*)

The voices of Ravish Naik are impenetrable. Beware, I tell you, the end is near! Now my disciples will pass among you to receive your offerings and mark you with the sword of Ravish Naik.

Some rather moronic-looking followers ringing small bells pass through the crowd with bowls. Others mark the foreheads of the donors with a red felt tip pen. Some begin to undress to jeers from the crowd. Women offer up their babies in supplication.

PREACHER

The end is near. You must submit! Ravish Naik speaks through me. Yes, night is drawing near. All will be defeated and the sword of judgement will divide the just from the unjust, virtue from ignominy. Yes, you heard what I said. Ignominy. Submit!

A wave of astonishment surges through the crowd as columns of pigeons rise noisily into the air in a fluster of wings, their scattered calligraphy recomposing to form an apparently smiling face.

The stunned face of the preacher.

Terrorised, the screaming crowds disperse. In the panic, a pram escapes and trundles towards the steps which it begins to descend, gathering speed as it goes. Miraculously it is halted half-way down by a distant gesture from Eric.

A police helicopter flies through the face formed by the pigeons.

The co-pilot leans out to look down at the scattering crowd and sees that it too composes a face.

The co-pilot takes photographs of the scene.

Employment Agency Waiting Room – Int. – Day
Among those waiting their turn are Michèle and Antoine; they converse in hushed voices, leaning against a message board.

ANTOINE
But you know, that's not the way I see it … they're all pretty sickening, but if you want to know it's Robert who really makes me puke. I mean, you have to take responsibility...

MICHÈLE
Oh darling, you're so right!

ANTOINE (*mechanically picking up a newspaper from an empty chair*)
Hey, check this out!

Two large photos appear on the front page, one of the crowd, the other of the pigeons, each forming the shape of a face.

Above them runs the headline: PANIC AT OST PARK.

MICHÈLE
What is it?

ANTOINE
It's their cosmic muppet again!

A female head pops up above the message board. The woman listens with interest to everything they say.

ANTOINE
It can take whatever form it wants, one minute it's in the sky, the next in the crowd, but it's the same thing. It can appear in a freak weather front, in radio interference, in anything... That thing is dangerous.

MICHÈLE
Yes, but one day ... someone's going to nail them.

ANTOINE
Sshh, not so loud! Someone might hear.

A number appears on the screen.

MICHÈLE
27, isn't that us?

ANTOINE
Yes, it's our turn, come on!

Lab – Int. – Day

Naked, Axel is doing pushups.

AXEL
17, 18, 19, 20, 21...

UIQ punctuates his movements with a rhythmic chanting.

Janice looks at him, laughs and undresses. She approaches him but he pushes her away.

AXEL
Don't get me wrong, I'm not gay or anything. But you know how it is with women...

She shrugs and moves away. He gets up and lunges at her, bites one of her buttocks causing her to cry out. He leaps on top of her and pins her to the ground.

As their gestures become more and more erotic, Eric falls into a catatonic stupor.

UIQ stops singing and begins signalling to Manou, drawing her attention to what is going on between Axel and Janice.

Manou shrugs with a knowing air.

MANOU
So what? Leave them to it.

UIQ groans.

As though they were alone, Janice and Axel dance around the room caressing each other, while UIQ like a disgruntled infant makes a series of despairing grimaces.

MANOU (*to UIQ*)
What...? What's up with you?

UIQ, its pathetic expression unchanging, tries to make her understand its unease.

AXEL
Stop! Wait a sec...

He leans over Janice, who smiles at him in extreme close-up.

On the screen UIQ's face smiles in the exact same way.

As Janice and Axel go on caressing, we see UIQ assume the expressions of ecstasy of one and the other in turn. We hear it moan with pleasure.

Immobile as a statue, Eric stands on a chair, pointing his finger towards some invisible object.

Under the bed sheets, Axel and Janice's excitement rises, as on the screen UIQ's face goes into convulsions. Suddenly it emits a dreadful guttural cry, like that of some animal, a cry that seems interminable.

Axel leaps up, furious and panicked. UIQ's cry begins to die away to a pitiful lament.

AXEL (*extremely angry*)
I've had it with this shit! What's up with him?

MANOU (*to Axel*)
You're not nice to him...

The monkey goes crazy and begins jumping from machine to machine, finally landing on Eric who doesn't move a muscle even when the animal defecates down his shirt.

Janice gets dressed.

JANICE (*to UIQ*)
Calm down, it's okay, they're going... We can talk now, you know, talk ... just you and me.

Axel, still upset, hurriedly puts his clothes on.

AXEL
I've fucking had it with you two!

He leaves, followed by Manou carrying the monkey.

Janice moves closer to UIQ on the screen, who continues to groan. Eric is still standing on the stool.

JANICE
Listen, you're gonna have to help me here ... otherwise I can't help you. What's wrong? You know what I think, I think you're jealous...

UIQ
Jealous? *Je loss?*

JANICE
Yes, jealous.

UIQ
So it's a question of body, of flesh, skin, possession...

Factory – Int. – Evening

Sitting at the foot of the metal staircase leading to the laboratory, Manou converses with UIQ through her headset.

MANOU

What? What did you say? We're going to give him something special ... tell me again, what do I have to put in it?

UIQ (*off*)

Glucose, potassium chloride, dl-tocopherol acetate, vitamin E, ephynal...

MANOU

What's that?

UIQ (*off*)

Look in the drug cabinet. It's a bottle of little pills. You just have to crush them to a powder.

Kitchen – Int. – Evening

Manou opens the drug cabinet, but the monkey, much faster than her, grabs the bottles she's looking for. She gives it a smack. Then she begins emptying the different bottles into a mortar, grinding the contents down into a powder that she then dilutes with water before pouring the mixture through a coffee filter.

FRED

What are you cooking up there?

MANOU

Nothing to do with you.

She takes the monkey.

FRED (*indicating the whitish mixture in the cafetiere*)

You going to give her that?

MANOU
What do you think I am? I'm not mad, you know!

FRED
Stay here, Lara!

He tries to take back the monkey, but it attaches itself to Manou.

<u>Factory – Ext. / Int. – Evening</u>

We follow the girl into the courtyard.

MANOU (*to UIQ*)
What do you want me to do? I'm scared.

UIQ (*off*)
No... I'm sure you're very happy! You like playing doctor, don't you.

Manou enters the dark hangar. She turns on a small torch. In the beam we see the tramp, lying dead drunk among piles of rubbish.

UIQ (*off*)
Go on.

MANOU
What if he wakes up?

UIQ (*off*)
Gently does it.

Manou carefully empties the contents of the cafetiere into a half-empty wine bottle.

MANOU
Eugh! It's disgusting!

The tramp stirs in his sleep, Manou switches off the torch. He grumbles in the dark, we hear him grab the bottle and guzzle down its contents.

<u>Street – Ext. – Evening</u>

The street is almost deserted. Michèle and Antoine walk hand in hand along the sidewalk.

ANTOINE
You remember that Kipling poem … how does it go again?

MICHÈLE
You mean the story about what it is to be a man?

ANTOINE
That's it: "If you can … watch the things you gave your life to, broken...

A car pulls up alongside them, shrieking to a halt.

ANTOINE
...and lose, and start at your beginnings, and never breathe a word about your loss... you'll be a man, my son."

I wish I'd had a father who spoke to me like that.

Two men get out of the car, grab the teenagers and bundle them into the back seat. The car takes off.

Hangar – Int. – Day

Under the glare of a white light, the tramp lies on the ground, connected to a drip, he seems to be in a dreadful state. Manou goes up to him and lifts one of his eyelids, shuddering with revulsion.

MANOU (*to UIQ, through the headset*)
He's going to die, isn't he?

UIQ (*off*)
Oh no, on the contrary...

She gets up on tiptoe to try to stop the drip, but as she's not tall enough, she has to step onto the tramp's body which emits a grumbling sound. She regulates the drip with precision as the monkey roots around in the garbage, eating whatever it can find.

MANOU (*to UIQ*)
What do I do now?

UIQ (*off*)
Whatever you like. Why not take his temperature?

MANOU
Eugh, disgusting pig!

UIQ
Listen to his heart.

Manou picks up a stethoscope and places it on the tramp's chest.

MANOU
I can't hear anything.

UIQ (*off*)
It's true it hasn't got much of a beat, but it's interesting nonetheless.

She looks at the tramp. He is clearly in a very bad way.

MANOU
I'm going to call the doctor.

UIQ (*off*)
No, there's no point. Put the biopastilles on him!

MANOU
The what?

UIQ
You know, the little sweets.

MANOU
Where?

UIQ (*off*)
Here and there. All over.

Hesitant at first, Manou finally obeys, placing pastilles at certain precise points on the tramp's body: three in triangular formation on the cheek, others on the chest and arms.

<u>Lab – Int. – Day</u>

Janice sits next to the screen, as she speaks to UIQ.

UIQ
Come closer, it's important. Touch my face with yours.

Janice places her head against the blurred face, which makes her own face glow, outlining it with a shimmering halo.

UIQ
You know, I'm actually very aware of all the ... stress I've put you through. But you must admit, it wasn't easy for me to get to the point I am now. It's thanks to you if I've managed. And now I'm going to stop being a nuisance. I've found a radical solution that will change everything...

JANICE
What?

UIQ
It's difficult to say... It's something that all humans no doubt experience at some time in their lives ... but for me it is unique. Janice, I love you absolutely and I want us to be ... married. You'll see from now on, everything will be different, I swear!

This infantile phase is complete, I am done with it and now you can really count on me. You, your friends, humanity. There are many things I can do. I can do everything.

JANICE
And what do you plan to do?

UIQ
Well, I don't know, maybe an AIDS vaccine, a solution to global famine, eradication of world pollution, all the pollution...

JANICE
Okay, great, but what about this marriage business? You want a real wedding? With flowers? And a priest? Who's going to be your best man?

She bursts into laughter.

UIQ
Don't laugh, I beg you, don't laugh at me!

JANICE
Don't take it the wrong way. It's not you after all.

UIQ
I'll take care of everything.

<u>Hangar – Int. – Day</u>

The tramp wakes up and utters a last gasp, before he slumps down dead.

Distraught, Manou gathers up her headset and runs away. The camera follows her as she makes her way back to the kitchen.

<u>Kitchen – Int. –Day</u>

Robert is wired up to Fred, Steve, Axel and Jennifer. Manou arrives, in a state of shock.

JENNIFER
What happened honey?

Manou doesn't respond. She starts to cry.

ROBERT
What are you crying about? Christ, you can be a pain sometimes...

MANOU (*between sobs*)
It wasn't my fault...

JENNIFER
Fault, what fault ... explain?

MANOU (*crying as she speaks*)
It's because he's dead.

STEVE
Who's dead? Who are you talking about?

MANOU
I don't know. You don't know him, it's not my fault... I didn't want him to die.

ROBERT
Go and play, it's nothing.

Axel's ears prick up as he hears a muffled sound from a room nearby. He gets up and heads to Janice's room.

Janice's Space – Int. – Day

Axel confirms that the noises are real. There is undoubtedly someone in the room. He opens the door a crack to peer in.

A close-up of Axel reveals his angered surprise. He kicks open the door and we glimpse the back of a man who doesn't turn round. Axel leaps at the intruder who deftly steps aside to watch Axel sail past him and crash to the floor with a cry of pain.

STRANGER (*off*)
You okay?

Axel looks at him, nonplussed.

AXEL (*stammering*)
Who the fuck are you? What are you doing there? Are you from the feds? You've no right to be here. And that's my tie!

We don't have a complete view of the intruder's face, which only serves to increase the air of mystery and fascination that surrounds him. He undoes the tie and hands it back to Axel.

AXEL (*stuttering*)
My shirt, trousers...

STRANGER
Sorry old boy, it's not exactly the tropics...

AXEL
Who are you?

STRANGER
I came to see Janice.

He goes out of the room. Axel follows him, dazed.

Kitchen – Int. – Day

As the unknown visitor enters, the room falls silent. Standing behind him, Axel seems frozen.

ROBERT (*to Axel, extremely worried*)
What does he want? Is he a cop?

AXEL
I don't think so.

ROBERT (*to the stranger*)
Who are you?

Before the stranger has time to reply, Manou goes up to him and observes him from below. In extreme close-up, we see a triangle of beauty spots on his cheek.

STRANGER
Don't mind me. Is there any coffee?

He goes over to the cupboard.

STEVE
Help yourself! Like us to rustle you up a full English breakfast?

STRANGER
Who wants one?

MANOU
I'd like one.

He takes Manou in his arms and lifts her up, so she can get the coffee filters from the top shelf. Manou leans against his cheek, stroking the beauty spots with a finger.

MANOU
What are those?

He looks at her straight in the eye. Manou bursts into a fit of giggles.

MANOU (*raising her arms to be lifted again*)
Again! Again!

He lifts her up.

ROBERT
What do you want here?

STRANGER
I'm here to see Janice.

MANOU
Come with me.

Manou jumps into the man's arms and once again puts her hand on his beauty spots.

MANOU
Why don't you want to tell them?

STRANGER
Tell them what?

MANOU
You know perfectly well what!

He puts his finger in her mouth and strokes her teeth.

MANOU (*freeing herself*)
You dirty old man.

JENNIFER
What are you doing with her? Let her go.

STRANGER
Nothing untoward, I assure you. Worry not.

Manou unbuttons his shirt.

STRANGER
What are you up to?

MANOU
Just looking at something.

A gentle struggle ensues.

MANOU
Yes, that's it!
(*To the others*) I'm going to take him to see Janice.

Everybody looks stunned.

We follow Manou and the stranger to the laboratory entrance.

MANOU
What's your name?

STRANGER
Whatever you want. What would you like it to be?

MANOU
Umm, I don't know... Artichoke, no, that's not a proper name ... how about Bruno. Bruno, do you like it?

BRUNO
Okay, Bruno it is then. Bruno Artichoke!

She laughs.

MANOU (*indicating the trap door at the top of the stairs*)
It's there!

He tries to open it only to find it blocked.

MANOU (*to Janice*)
Hey, Janice! It's Bruno.

JANICE (*off*)
Bruno?

MANOU
Bruno Artichoke!

A church organ fills the building with the strains of Chopin's wedding march.

International Commission HQ – Ext./Int.– Day

A young uniformed policewoman walks through the revolving doors carrying a tray of cream cakes.

She carries the tray to an office where we find Michèle and Antoine surrounded by the President, the Spokesman and assorted bureaucrats and military men.

PRESIDENT
Ah, ammunition. Help yourselves, please. Now, let me see if I have this clear. So what you're saying is that this ... extraterrestrial amuses itself by creating interference, television, air traffic control and so on... But have you seen it? Michèle, what about you?

MICHÈLE (*hesitating*)
Yes, I think so.

PRESIDENT
Yes or no?

ANTOINE
Yes, Mr. President. We have.

SPOKESMAN
You saw it? You touched it?

ANTOINE
No, no, it's not like that.

MICHÈLE
You can never touch it.

PRESIDENT
Calm down, listen my young friends. This extra-terrestrial …
how did it find its way here?

Antoine and Michèle give a shrug.

PRESIDENT
Is it armed?

ANTOINE
No, Sir.

OFFICER
So it can't be dangerous then?

MICHÈLE
Oh yes, because it can take any form it wants.

ANTOINE
And sometimes it goes completely crazy...

OTHER MAN
Crazy?

POLICEMAN
So how about we take a gander down at the factory, Mr. President?

PRESIDENT
Relax, superintendent! For the moment there are to be no fireworks. We don't want another Brussels, do we? The way I see it, we must exercise extreme caution.

SPOKESMAN
If I may ask, Mr. President...

PRESIDENT
What is it?

SPOKESMAN
How do you see the situation?

The president gives a shrug and bites into a cream cake.

Factory – Lab Staircase – Int. – Day

The whole community is gathered at the foot of the metal staircase below the trap door, anxiously listening for strange noises.

ROBERT
We have to go in, we can't leave her with him.

He tries to shoulder open the trap door but only succeeds in injuring himself.

ROBERT
Ow!

AXEL
Wait, I can try to get in by the window.

<u>Factory – Ext./Int. – Day</u>

Axel scales the facade of the building and hoists himself up onto the roof terrace. He goes to the window and presses his face against the glass.

Janice sees him.

JANICE
I thought I told you to stay out of my way!

AXEL
Are you ok? What's going on?

JANICE
It's fine. It's fine, now go.

UIQ (*anxious, to Janice*)
What's the problem now? I don't understand. I'm there now … there I am, in flesh and blood. We can finally get married. It's wonderful!

JANICE (*to UIQ*)
Shut that fucking face, you're sick! Sick in the head except you don't have a head. It's crazy, what you're suggesting. Fucking gaga. I should have known. Oh fuck, I should have known. But who would believe any of this shit?

She starts to kick the machines. Bruno switches the oscilloscope off. UIQ's face disappears. Janice calms down.

JANICE (*to Bruno*)
Look, it's not you. I've nothing against ... you. But this ... this procedure... It's unbearable. I can't... I see now what a mistake this has been, for months I was sucked in, but now it's clear. Incredible. Every time, it was never enough, he always wanted more. He just used me up. I think I must be going mad.

BRUNO (*whose face remains hidden*)
You're right. What can I say? The whole situation is ... completely warped... I understand you... I'm going.

JANICE
Where? Where the fuck are you gonna go?

BRUNO
It doesn't matter where.

Janice turns to look at him, with an expression of almost unbearable intensity.

Factory – Ext. – Day

A car draws up alongside the factory buildings. Inside are the Commision president, a police officer and Antoine and Michèle, both of whom look tense and ill at ease.

MICHÈLE (*pointing at the building*)
It's there.

The president presses his nose up to the glass, scrutinizes the metal gate and tries to see into the dilapidated courtyard beyond.

PRESIDENT
That's where they're hiding out?

ANTOINE
Yes, I mean behind there.

PRESIDENT
Well, we don't want to give ourselves away quite so soon, do we Driver...

POLICE OFFICER (*into a walkie-talkie*)
Order all vehicles to take up discreet positions following plan A and to stay on guard! Marksmen to keep out of sight and not to engage until the order is given ... understood?

We see armed men scurrying across the roof of a nearby building, taking up their positions while others scan the factory through binoculars. Several unmarked cars pull up outside the factory.

Janice's Space – Int. – Day

Naked under the shower, Bruno rinses his body. As the soap bubbles dissolve, we gradually discover a series of beauty spots forming the same pattern as the "pastilles" on the body of the tramp.

Janice, also naked, throws him a towel. Bruno rubs himself dry, while Janice approaches him and starts to caress his beauty spots.

173

JANICE
What are these? They're amazing!

Bruno lifts the hair from the back of her neck and leans forward to breathe in her smell.

BRUNO
No, this is amazing!

For the first time we see Bruno's face.

Suddenly, a glow invades the screen, merely colours at first, then a face, that of UIQ.

Janice looks alternately at one and the other.

JANICE
How do you two work it out between yourselves?

BRUNO
Simple. He is him and I'm me.

JANICE
Yes, but who does what?

Bruno takes her in his arms.

BRUNO
I do everything.

UIQ gives him the finger.

JANICE
And what about me, what the fuck has this got to do with me?

Bruno traces a hyperbole of n dimensions on the screen. A trellis of lines appears across which we see a point of light moving rapidly.

BRUNO
You see the point? The point is you.

JANICE (*alarmed*)
And where's the way out of this system of yours?

BRUNO
That, my dear, is another story...

JANICE (*to UIQ*)
No, it's a fucking nightmare!

The sound of organ music returns.

BRUNO (*to UIQ*)
Easy on the bass pedals!

(*To Janice*) Say, this is all very nice, but I'm getting a bit hungry...

JANICE
I'll go and look for something. Wait here. Do you want something to drink? Wine, beer...?

BRUNO (*turning towards UIQ*)
How about some Beaujolais?

A list of different vintages and producers scrolls down UIQ's forehead.

A 1976 Morgon Côte du Py?

JANICE
What do you think this is? Claridges? You'll just have to take what we've got.

She quickly gets dressed and goes out shrugging her shoulders. Bruno gets into bed and makes himself comfortable. He lights a cigarette and grabs a copy of "Road Runner."

UIQ *starts to cough.*
(*indicating the magazine*) Why are you reading that crap?

BRUNO
What do you know, imbecile? I like looking at the images, purely for the beauty of the forms, not the performance. I don't give a shit about the rest of it.

UIQ
It is nonetheless rather irritating.

Kitchen – Int. – Day

Janice opens all the cupboards. They're empty.

AXEL
So?

JANICE
So what? What's up with you? Why the long face?

Axel goes back to where Steve is working, composing different systems of algorithms on the computer screen.

JANICE
You could do the shopping once in a while.

AXEL
Robert has the flu.

Factory – Ext. – Day

Janice descends the hillside road. We see her image framed by binoculars, unseen eyes that discreetly follow her at a distance.

Suddenly a motorbike screeches to a halt at her feet, narrowly avoiding ploughing into her.

HELMUT
Get on!

JANICE
Hey Lone Ranger!

Helmut honks a strangely musical-sounding horn. Janice smiles and gets on behind him.

Car – Ext./ Int. – Day

POLICEMAN
Get the registration. I want to know who that biker is!

Janice's Space – Int. – Night

Lying on the bed, Bruno puffs nervously on a cigarette.

UIQ
Where is she?

BRUNO
Gone shopping.

UIQ
Why doesn't she come back?

BRUNO
Stop whining, she'll be back!

UIQ
You don't care, say it? You don't give a shit either way.

BRUNO
No, don't say that.

UIQ
You don't know what it is … to suffer.

BRUNO
That's rich coming from you. After what you've put me through.

UIQ
It's not the same. I'm talking about real suffering, absolute suffering. No, you don't know what that is!

BRUNO
In any case you always know everything.

UIQ
Yes, everything. So what if I do? You want to know what else? They've got us surrounded.

BRUNO
Who?

UIQ
The feds. There's a whole army of them. On the roofs, they're everywhere!

BRUNO
We have to warn the others.

UIQ
Let's go look for Janice.

BRUNO
Janice, I don't know where she's gone.

UIQ
Oh, that's easy. She's gone back to the club, with her shitty friends.

BRUNO
Ok, let's go.

<u>Road – Ext. – Night</u>

The van is followed at a discreet distance by an unmarked police car. Axel is at the wheel, Bruno beside him, with UIQ no more than a voice-off that speaks in counterpoint to Bruno.

UIQ (*off*)
Step on it!

BRUNO
Cool it, will you.

AXEL
What is it? I can't go any faster. Where's the fire?

UIQ
Not the fire. The feds!

Axel looks in the rear-view mirror and sees the car following them at a distance.

AXEL
I'll take care of this.

He steps on the gas. A chase ensues. After shaking off their pursuers, they dump the van and continue on foot.

Bruno and Axel walk along the edge of a canal.

UIQ (*off, to Bruno*)
Why did you let her go? Answer me!

Bruno walks in a reluctant hurry as though he were being pushed from behind. As they break into a run, he overtakes Axel and knocks over a woman who topples a parked scooter as she falls. At that moment a lorry arrives and screetches to a halt.

BRUNO (*to UIQ*)
Careful shithead!

Outraged, the woman turns to face him.

BRUNO
I'm sorry, but...

UIQ (*off*)
This is no time for gallantry, get a move on!

The woman looks on, dumbstruck.

Club – Int. – Night

Cold wave music. The club is packed.

UIQ (*off*)
Where is she? What do you see?

BRUNO
Nothing, I don't see her.

UIQ (*off*)
Then look. Use your eyes. I'm telling you she's here some-where, I know it.

Bruno mingles with the crowd. Axel grabs him by the shoulder.

AXEL (*to Bruno*)
Hey, take it easy man, let's get a drink.

Axel and Bruno sit down at a table

UIQ (*off*)
I know perfectly well what's going on! She's, she's canoodling with someone, isn't she, the trollop!

We see Janice dancing close with Helmut on the dancefloor. UIQ sends a shock through Bruno who tries to stand up and collapses back onto his seat.

UIQ (*off*)
Do something! Go on, or I'll tear the whole place apart.

BRUNO
She can dance if she wants!

The waiter approaches the table to take their order.

UIQ (*off*)
Smash the bastard's fucking face in!

Astonished face of the waiter.

AXEL (*to the waiter*)
Beat it. We're ok for the moment...

He gets up and goes to look for Janice on the dancefloor. He grabs her by the wrist, pushing Helmut away.

AXEL (*whispering in her ear*)
I really think you should come with me.

JANICE
What? What's going on?

AXEL
It's Bruno, I mean UIQ. I think they have some issues to sort out!

JANICE
Frankly they can go fuck each other, for all I care.

She grabs Helmut's arm and drags him towards the exit.

AXEL
And the feds are on our ass!

UIQ (*off*)
What are you waiting for? Go on. Do him!

BRUNO
I told you, no.

UIQ (*off*)
Mash the fucker to a pulp!

All of a sudden, we hear screams from a group of youths gathered around a video-game that begins flashing dementedly.

<u>Club – Ext. – Night</u>

Janice and Helmut walk along the canal, kissing. Suddenly Bruno looms up behind them. Sensing footsteps, Janice turns around.

JANICE (*to Helmut*)
Let's move.

She begins to walk faster.

BRUNO (*to UIQ*)
I'm not going to let you do that. It's revolting, what you're suggesting.

UIQ (*off*)
Don't you get it? He's going to stick it in!

The streetlamps along the road begin to buzz and flicker as though affected by an electromagnetic storm, their light fluctuating violently in rhythm and intensity. In a series of stroboscopic flashes we see Axel running after Bruno.

A truck comes juddering along the roadside behind him. It mounts the sidewalk and brushes Axel, who has just enough time to throw himself out of its path.

In the cabin, the driver looks with alarm at the crazily spinning dials of his instrument panel which emit a light strong enough to momentarily blind him.

We hear the sound of the shattering windscreen as he loses control of the vehicle which zigzags wildly, skims past Bruno and narrowly avoids crushing Janice and her companion, before it veers onto the bridge over the canal, crashes through the wooden barrier and plunges into the water.

Axel observes the accident, aghast, under the infernal din of the streetlamps.

BRUNO (*to UIQ*)
Enough of this bullshit!

UIQ (*off*)
Faster!

BRUNO (*still running*)
No, I won't do it!

He comes up behind Janice and Helmut brandishing a switch-blade. Janice tries to block his path with her body but he shoves her out of the way and leaps upon the youth, stabbing him multiple times with the knife.

Janice looks on in horror.

Axel arrives running, grabs Janice and tells her to run for it.

Bruno gazes down like a madman upon the inert body lying stretched out on the pavement.

BRUNO (*to UIQ*)
You bastard, you fuck, you fucking murderer!

He throws the knife away and stares disorientedly at the lights that continue to flicker and glow violently.

BRUNO (*to UIQ*)
You're finished motherfucker!

Your puppet-master days are over. I'm going to cut your fucking strings.

UIQ groans heavily.

UIQ (*off*)
It's not my fault! She doesn't love me anymore. You don't know how unhappy I am. Please. You have to help me. Please!

BRUNO (*to UIQ*)
You could have sorted this out fifty-thousand other ways!

UIQ (*off*)
Oh I don't lack means, that's for sure. But that's only in science and technology. As for these feelings, these ... passions, I don't know what to do with them, I'm lost. She doesn't love me anymore. Janice doesn't love me anymore. You don't know what that means, you'll never understand. My suffering. My suffering is incommensurable. And it's never going to end. Never.

BRUNO (*to UIQ*)
Oh, get over yourself!

He runs off as little by little the lights begin to dim.

Street – Ext. – Night

All vehicles have come to a standstill, their headlamps no longer working. Dragging Janice by the arm, Axel wrenches open a car door and hauls the driver out of his seat, taking his place.

AXEL (*to driver*)
Fuck off, this is an emergency!

He speeds off, glancing in the rear-view mirror, where he sees an abandoned infant still strapped into a baby-seat. He reverses the car, steering with one hand while loosening the child's belt with the other.

AXEL (*to driver*)
Here, don't forget your sprog!

Just as he is about to drive off, Bruno arrives running. Headlamps off, Axel hits the accelerator, slaloming wrecklessly to avoid obstacles, climbing onto the sidewalk and tipping the car onto two wheels before regaining traction and speeding off down the road.

As he approaches the factory, he sees the road ahead blocked by brasiers. He slams on the brakes.

POLICEMAN
You can't go that way!

AXEL
Why, what's happening?

POLICEMAN
None of your concern!

ANOTHER POLICEMAN
Who are you? Licence and registration please!

Manou descends from the back of a police van where we see all the other squatters except Eric. She walks up to Axel.

MANOU
Ah there you are, I'm coming with you.

She gets into the car as the police look on, speechless. Axel reverses violently, opening Janice's door.

AXEL
Get out! It's too dangerous. Take Manou!

MANOU
No, I want to go with you!

Before she can finish her sentence, Janice already has her out of the car.

JANICE (*to Manou*)
Where are the others?

Manou points towards the van.

Factory – Int. / Ext. – Night

At a window, armed with his mirror, Eric channels a beam of light towards the marksmen hidden in the courtyard. The light casts a faint reflection that skitters across the space until it alights upon the helmet of one of them, at which point it unleashes a luminous bolt of unbearable intensity. The shooter howls in pain, dropping his weapon and raising his hands to cover his face.

Shots ring out, the mirror shatters in pieces. Eric gathers up several shards that he manipulates to produce more beams, unleashing further bolts of intense light.

POLICEMAN
Cease fire. Fall back!

The marksmen retreat from their positions as Axel arrives on the scene.

POLICEMAN
What are you doing here?

AXEL
None of your fucking business!

A bolt narrowly misses him.

AXEL (*to Eric*)
Stop playing the infant. Let me come in.

As soon as he recognizes Axel's voice, Eric lays down his shards of mirror and scoops up Fred's monkey which he begins to cradle in his arms. Axel climbs up the building façade, bursting into the lab through the window.

ERIC (*indicating the mirror*)
Francis ... he's there...

UIQ (*off*)
And Dominique ... they killed her.

ERIC
It's not true, it's not true. What are you saying?

UIQ (*off*)
Francis and Dominique, they killed them both.

ERIC
Shut up, what do you know? They're both here with me.

UIQ (*off, screaming*)
They're dead, I tell you. Dead!

AXEL
Both of you, calm down. Enough with this bullshit. Now's not the time. Get yourselves sorted. We have to get out of here.

UIQ (*off, screaming*)
Get out? You've got to be shitting me. No way are we leaving now. The fuckers capped Francis!

Suddenly, UIQ appears in the form of a human-sized hologram.

AXEL
Listen, it's okay. We're going to set everything up again someplace else.

UIQ
What? You want to separate Janice and me?

AXEL
It won't be for long. Just the time to find a quieter place...

UIQ
But I don't want to leave her.

AXEL
Don't worry! She'll be there!

UIQ
Where is Janice? Why isn't she here?

AXEL
She had to leave. There are cops everywhere!

UIQ
I don't give a fuck about the cops!

AXEL
Just stop it! Haven't you caused enough trouble?

Suddenly, beside the hologram, UIQ appears again on the large screen in the form of the face. The two materialisations of the Infra-quark Universe speak at the same time.

UIQ
Dominique! They've killed Dominique!

He moans.

AXEL
Listen, you're super-intelligent right, so you should be able to compute that we are in a world of shit. You have to help me, otherwise we're toast. Is that what you want?

UIQ (*hologram*)
You have to help me. What you are asking would be a catastrophe for me. If I am separated from Janice, it's as though she were dead. Because if she's gone, I ... I won't be able to find this ... this me that I am with her.

AXEL
You're wrong. Don't worry, it'll be fine.

UIQ
You really want to break the contact?

AXEL
Let me finish and listen to what I'm saying. I'll start again using the same strain as relay (*he indicates the sample*). I'll set up a new lab...

UIQ
And will Janice be there?

AXEL
I promise you, she'll be there.

UIQ
And Steve, Jennifer, the others? Manou?

AXEL
I guarantee it!

UIQ
Because if I lose Janice, it will be horrible, more horrible than any human could possibly imagine. I will be left with nothing but pain. And pain ... when you have no body, no way to locate it, limit it, and no way to die, no way to end...

AXEL
Yeah, I know all that. Come on!

UIQ
No wait... Don't leave ... me. What happened? I need to understand.

AXEL (*exasperated*)
Look, up to now we've managed to overcome all the problems, no? I mean what was it in the end? Just a bit of jealousy, that's all. It's nothing. I say we wait till everything's calmed down and next time we try and look at it from another angle.

UIQ (*hologram*)
Yes, from another angle. There should have been more humour in our relationship, other images. The guy I killed. It's serious, isn't it? I don't mean for him. He's of no account. But for Janice... Will she still love me after what I've done?

AXEL
Look, forget about that for now!

ERIC
No, they haven't killed Francis and Dominique.

(*He brandishes two pieces of mirror*). Look, they're here.

AXEL (*to Eric*)
Listen Eric, you have to help me, I need you. Don't make it any more complicated, please. You have to stop dreaming!

Eric flips. Suddenly he starts to speak normally, with authority.

ERIC (*to the UIQ hologram*)
Come on, we have to go. You bring Dominique and I'll take Francis.

(*He holds up the two slivers of mirror*) You see them?

192

UIQ (*hologram*)
Yes, I see them.

ERIC
Alright, so get them. And we'll meet downstairs.

Bruno bursts into the laboratory. Reeling, almost beside himself with rage, he shoves Axel violently out of the way and lunges at the bacteria sample. Axel tries to prevent him, Bruno throws him to the ground with incredible force and grabs a Bunsen burner. He lights up the burner and torches the sample.

AXEL
No, don't do it!

Both UIQ's hologram and its face are consumed in a garland of rosy flames. Eric grabs a hammer and hits Bruno on the head from behind. Bruno spins around and turns the burner on Eric's hand, making him drop the hammer. Eric responds immediately with a series of vicious headbutts.

AXEL (*to Eric*)
Forget him. Come on!

The laboratory catches fire. Trapped by the flames, the monkey emits a series of high pitched squeals as it burns. From the court-yard we hear the stampede of boots and the sound of weapons being cocked as the police mount another charge.

AXEL
Eric, come on!

Eric ignores him. With his clothes on fire, he continues to hit Bruno who gradually weakens. Dawn begins to break as Axel makes his escape across the roofs of the burning factory buildings.

International Commission – Int. – Day

In the control room, the whole complex apparatus of screens and computers lies deserted. The commission members are gathered around a nearby table, listening intently to the President.

PRESIDENT
Gentlemen, it seems that all disturbances have now ceased. Nonetheless I suggest you continue to exercise the utmost vigilance.

MEMBER OF THE COMMISSION
Certainly, Mr. President.

ANOTHER MEMBER
Yes, but why if you say we've nailed it?

PRESIDENT
Well, currently we are seeing an alarming rise in the incidence of ... heu ... of purpura.

He turns towards a scientist.

SCIENTIST
It's a vascular illness, usually quite benign, but what we're seeing now appears to be a new strain we've never encountered before.

PRESIDENT
We'll have to alert the WHO!

SCIENTIST
But Mr. President, they are the ones who actually contacted us; they can't figure out what's causing this bizarre epidemic.

ANOTHER EXPERT
Mr. President, I should tell you that what we are witnessing is an altogether exceptional phenomenon. Let me show you something.

The expert presents a series of photos of afflicted people whose faces are covered in marks that themselves take the form of a face.

The commission members look shocked as they recognizing the face of UIQ the way it had appeared on the TV screens.

PRESIDENT
Yes, it is as you say, bizarre. Quite bizarre.

Apartment – Int. – Day

In a bare room Jennifer sits in lotus position. Manou arrives and kneels down, hugging Jennifer and laying her head on her shoulder. Jennier interrupts her meditation and speaks softly to the child.

JENNIFER
What is it?

MANOU
Where's Janice?

JENNIFER
I don't know. She'll be back.

Manou slips her hand under Jennifer's sweatshirt and moves it across her back. Feeling something odd, she stops.

MANOU
What's that?

Jennifer tries to reach round to touch her back. Unable to reach the spot, she removes her sweatshirt and goes to look in a mirror. She screams, as she perceives what appear to be scales growing out of her spine.

Hospital – Int. – Day

We see the clenched face of a convulsing infant which a doctor covers in an oxygen mask. The body of the child resembles that of a fish. Another doctor enters the room brandishing a sheet of paper.

DOCTOR
It's the opposite of what we thought. Hyper-oxygenation.

The doctor removes the oxygen mask from the baby who, of its own accord, jumps into a nearby bathtub. The doctor opens the taps. As the bath fills the baby begins to leap and frolic like a salmon.

Hospital – Ext. – Day

Several ambulances converge in front of the emergency department. Stretchers bearing men, women and children, their heads submerged in basins of water, are carried into the hospital.

DOCTOR
It's amazing, the speed at which their lungs transform themselves into gills.

NURSE
What's even more shocking is how these new mutants seems to have become impervious to fatigue, heat, cold, even pain.

DOCTOR
That's probably the result of excess endorphins. We'll have to alter the dosage.

International Commission – Int. – Day

The spokesman sits behind his desk. A secretary hydrates him constantly with a large sponge.

SPOKESMAN
...Believe me when I say I understand your situation and sympathize entirely. Now tell me again, quickly, what your demands are, because I don't have much time.

We see Robert, with the shaggy, drooping ears of a dog.

ROBERT (*barking*)
Look, it's not rocket science, and we're not backing down. This is what we want: closure of all isolation camps and dog pounds...

STEVE
Yes, it's completely illegal.

Steve has the eyes of a fly. The image he sees appears multiplied into myriad cells like a beehive.

ROBERT
Secondly, an end to all professional interdictions and sexual discrimination in the workplace. Third, we want bird perches in all lifts.

Several telephones begin to ring. The spokesman picks up one of the receivers.

SPOKESMAN
Hello! Yes, can you just hold on one moment? (*To the secretary*) Water, water, I'm drying up!

The secretary hydrates him with renewed dilligence. As a sign of thanks he taps her on the bottom with one of his tentacles.

SECRETARY
Oh! Mr Spokesman!

Outside in the corridor Robert and Steve prepare to leave. Fred hails them from a distance.

FRED
Steve! Robert!

They turn round.

FRED (*scrutinizing them*)
My god, you too!

STEVE
And what about you? Nothing?

Fred examines himself.

FRED
Not that I know of. For the moment at least!

ROBERT
You didn't see Jennifer?

A snail moves slowly along Robert's arm. Fred looks stupefied.

ROBERT
What the hell are you doing here anyway?

FRED (*secretively*)
We're working on it.

STEVE
How so brother?

ROBERT
Whatever it is you say you're doing, it amounts to a barrel of horseshit. And until we can make contact with UIQ, that's all it will ever be. That's what I told your head octopus.

FRED
Come with me. I'm so happy to see you guys. But here, for now everything's hush hush. Can I count on you?

STEVE
Whatever, man.

Flashing his electronic pass at some armed guards, he guides them through a maze of subterranean corridors.

FRED
Well what I can tell you is we've already re-established contact. We've managed to reconstitute the cyanobacteria and set up the lab again.

ROBERT
So why didn't you say so?

FRED
Because the situation hasn't changed. We can't get anything out of the obstinate little fuck.

They arrive at armour-plated doors.

FRED
Hello, this is Fred Newman, I'm with Robert Muhler and Steve Johnson...

VOICE-OFF
Who are they?

FRED
Two guys from the commune, old friends of UIQ. They could be useful.

VOICE-OFF
With the way things are right now I don't see why not. Ok, they can come in!

The automatic doors slide open. Inside are around fifteen people, technical experts and other members of the commission, several of them mutants. They turn towards Robert and Steve.

On the video screen of the electron microscope the familiar cellular corpuscles pulse with light. There is no other image.

FRED
Nothing new?

GUY
Nothing. We have contact, but that's about all.

STEVE
You sure it's UIQ? I mean you sure it's our main motherfucker.

FRED
It's him alright. No doubt about it.

He sits down in front of a microphone.

FRED

Listen, UIQ. Steve and Robert are here, you remember them, don't you want to say hello?

Superimposed upon the cellular blobs appear the words "No comment." Fred turns towards Steve and Robert.

FRED

It's eight days he's been like that. No comment, No fucking comment. It's all we can squeeze out of him.

Robert approaches the microphone.

ROBERT

UIQ, it's me, Robert. Listen we used to be friends didn't we. If you even remember what that means, you can't go on like this, you have to do something to get us out of this. Look what I've become. Look at my face. And look what you've done to Jennifer. You remember Jennifer, don't you? Well, take a look.

We hear the sound of quiet sniggering, as the blobs seem to form themselves into a face.

All those present in the room burst into a round of applause.

GUY

It reacted, it reacted!

ROBERT

What's with you?

FRED

He responded, we're in business.

ROBERT
You call that a response.

(*To UIQ*) Listen you little asswipe, there are millions of us here, all disfigured, mutilated, broken and you think it's a joke.

Once again the same phrase, "No comment," appears on the screen. The image goes back to how it was before.

The others are furious with Robert.

TECHNICIAN
You've screwed up everything! You mustn't talk to it like that.

ANOTHER TECHNICIAN
Laying a guilt trip on the little guy. If he keeps pulling shit like that we're fucked.

ROBERT
Hey, who do you think you're talking to, four-eyes. We're from the National Delegation of Mutants!

The technician signals him to shut up, lifting his shirt to reveal something we cannot see but which must be pretty horrible judging from Robert and Steve's reaction. Steve tries to stop himself from retching.

ROBERT
Oh well, if you put it like that, I'm sorry comrade.

(*To UIQ*) That amuses you too does it? Aren't you ashamed? It's intolerable, that's what it is. We demand you take whatever measures are necessary to restore each of us to ... to...

PATIENT
Their original look.

ROBERT
Yes, of course, their look!

EXPERT (*aside to Fred*)
Your buddy is a complete nutjob.

FRED (*irritated*)
No, he's a good guy. He's straight up and UIQ trusts him.

EXPERT (*to Robert*)
Thanks for your efforts. You've been a great help.

Steve pushes Robert out of the way to take his place.

STEVE
Look UIQ, I know where you're coming from. I got nothing to say to the contrary.

Close-up of Steve's fly-eyes, on whose facets we see multiplied images of members of the commission, many afflicted with mutations, holding their heads in despair.

STEVE
You did what you thought you had to do. And maybe in your place I would have been just as badass. But we have to rethink the situation here. We have to find another angle to approach it. Because what is this all about when you get down to it? Come on, we're among friends here so let's talk about it, you had a little episode, a little crisis...

On the facets of Steve's eyes, several commission members point their fingers to their temples to indicate a screw is loose.

203

STEVE
And you know jealousy, the good ol' green-eyed motherfucker, well that can lead to some pretty fucked up shit.

ROBERT
Yes, it always leads to the worst stupidities, starting with capitalism!

FRED
Wait … let Steve speak.

STEVE
You gotta listen up because what I gotta say to you now is going to sound like some pretty heavy shit. When you made contact with us, you were like … like a little baby, you thought it was all going to be easy as pie and it's true, what passed between us all, everything we did, it was some amazing shit. But then you fell in love with Janice and everything went ass up. And in a sense that was cool, it was the norm, you weren't prepared for it. I don't know how it goes down in your universe but here on planet Earth, love is always the kind of weird-ass shit that drives a motherfucker crazy.

All of a sudden, superimposed on the image of corpuscles there appear in quick succession a square, a circle, a triangle and then a single word "Janice," followed by a rapid blur of figures and algorithms. Everyone rises from their seat. The emotion in the room is intense.

EXPERT
Transmit those formulae to the decoding department immediately!

Hospital Corridor and Room – Int. – Day

Uniformed guards stand watch at the door to a hospital room. A nurse arrives pushing a trolley. One of them opens the door for her.

Inside is Janice dressed in a simple white bedshirt. Axel, seemingly in a state of collaspe, sits on the bed next to her.

In a corner of the room, the President of the commission paces up and down.

NURSE (*to Axel*)
I'm afraid you must leave now. I have to shave her.

AXEL
No, no way. I'm not going.

JANICE
If you don't mind I prefer to do it myself.

She grabs the shaving equipment.

NURSE
As you like.

The nurse goes out.

AXEL
You can't let them do it.

PRESIDENT (*to Axel*)
What option do we have? He says he will only speak to her, directly, and without intermediaries. This ... operation is the condition for returning things to normality. Bears thinking about, wouldn't you say? I cannot say how grateful we are that Miss Janice Cellini has agreed to this ... I won't say sacrifice ... no, to this magnificent act of boundless altruism!

JANICE (*wearily*)
Why don't you show your appreciation by shutting your trap.

PRESIDENT
Very well, very well.

AXEL
I can't accept this intervention. What you're suggesting, what you want to do to her is completely fucking crazy. We have to wait, however long it takes we just have to wait. UIQ needs us, he won't have any choice but to speak to us and when he does, everything will sort itself out. But this ... this intercerebral operation is just totally unacceptable...

PRESIDENT
Calm down, young man. I understand your feelings, you think we should wait but for how long? How many more mutations do you think can we cope with? You know how many there are per day right now? 17 million. I'm afraid we cannot afford to wait any longer. So...

(*He turns towards Janice*) It is a magnificent gesture that you have chosen to make, young lady, truly magnificent!

JANICE
If you think I give a shit about your 17 million freaks!

PRESIDENT
I understand how you feel, believe me, I do.

AXEL
You're right. What the hell do we care. Forget it. Let's get the fuck out of here!

PRESIDENT
Now wait a minute, we had an agreement...

JANICE
Don't worry grandpa. I'm not going to run out on you...

PRESIDENT
Thank you, speaking for all of us, thank you again.

JANICE
Now get the fuck out of my face.

The President retreats from the room.

PRESIDENT
Of course, of course.

Janice gets up, takes the electric razor and begins to shave her head in front of the mirror. Clumps of hair fall to the ground. Axel begins to cry.

JANICE
Leave it, Axel. Go. It's hard enough for me as it is. Don't make it any worse.

AXEL
Why are you giving in to this bullshit blackmail? We just have to wait until he calms down, that's all.

JANICE
You don't get it, do you? It's between him and me. He'll never accept anyone else interfering.

The door opens. An official enters bearing a sheaf of papers.

HOSPITAL OFFICIAL
If you just sign here and here... It's a pure formality.

JANICE
Give me the pen.

She signs.

JANICE
And now I want to be alone.

Bewildered and defeated, Axel allows himself to be led out of the room by the nurse and the official.

Hospital Corridor / Operating Theatre – Int. – Day

Asleep and her head-shaven, Janice is pushed on a trolley towards the operating theatre where the team of surgeons is ready. They examine a screen with an electronic diagram of the brain where we can see a large number of small luminous dots. A surgeon draws a grid pattern on Janice's skull.

Another surgeon manipulates a set of micro-implants with tiny pliers. Against the light, he observes the micro-implants shimmering in the test tubes. They look like some kind of iron filings.

SURGEON (*to his assistant*)
Christ! I wouldn't want that implanted in my noodle!

ASSISTANT
But tell me, professor ... will it be completely irreversible?

SURGEON
Of that there isn't the slightest doubt!

He raises his arms to the sky. They call him to start the operation.

SURGEON
Let's get this over with!

On a scanner we see sharp needles penetrating deeply into the brain.

<u>Hospital Room – Int. – Day</u>

In silence, Janice studies herself in a mirror. Her head, completey shorn, bears the scars of the recent operation,

She remains there motionless, very close to the mirror's surface, indifferent to the clouding of her breath. Extreme close-up of her eyes, the pupils dilated in an expression of extreme anguish.

A succession of shots of Janice, immobile in a chair, looking out the window. A stubble of hair beginning to sprout.

Behind her are Axel, Fred, Robert. They move their lips as if speaking but their words remain unheard.

<u>Hospital Garden – Ext. – Day</u>

Barefoot, Janice walks along a path wearing only a bedshirt. She runs her hand over her head, her hair still no more than a shadow of stubble.

JANICE
We're going home... What did he say? He'll be back tomorrow. What did he say? Tomorrow.

By the time she utters these last words, Janice's voice has completely changed. It's now a guttural, male voice.

Street – Ext. – Day

Strangely the road is deserted, sun blasted.

VOICE OFF (*monotonous but with occasional changes in timbre*) No, not now... They are still making noise... Do you hear? I should have told her... He had given it to me... Time for tea... It was higher... I'd have kept some... It goes on... Behind the door...

We realise it is Janice speaking as she walks.

JANICE
I didn't know... He came back... She will wash... He speaks to me... He's there I think... He'll be interested in that ... at home ... no, it's not my fault if I didn't tell her, it's that I didn't see him... I think I'm going ... it's not the same thing ... he did no wrong... But it's a long story, a long time ... leave me the bottle... I would have liked to...

She arrives at the road leading down to the factory.

They all left... It's not the same... We're going to give her... She has so many... I really wanted to... We will have the time... It annoys them... It doesn't matter... She didn't see anything... Maybe I'm expecting ... in that case ... it might change something... They'll have put up curtains ... there are eyes ... if you like...

She comes to the flat roof. We see that she is sweating despite having made almost no effort. With an impassive air, she unbuttons her bedshirt.

Wait ... we sorted them... I said so... No, not that... I remember... She looked at it...

Calmly, she walks along the edge.

It's possible ... he wanted ... I don't know where I put it ... he talked a lot ... to start over ... grey and blue...

Emotionless, she stares into space.

He would have... There's no reason... We can wait for him... It's possible.

She falls head first into the void.

We hear the dull crack of her body as it hits concrete.

A few seconds later, a pool of blood begins to form around her head. Silently she gets up, passes a hand over her skull and walks away.

(*Monotonous*) Might he give her back her death at least.

THE END

Univocal Publishing
123 North 3rd Street, #202
Minneapolis, MN 55401
www.univocalpublishing.com

ISBN 9781937561956

Jason Wagner, Drew S. Burk
(Editors)
All materials were printed and bound
in February 2016 at Univocal's atelier
in Minneapolis, USA.

This work was composed in Garamond and Trajan
The paper is Hammermill 98.
The letterpress cover was printed
on Crane's Lettra Pearl.
Both are archival quality and acid-free.